Positive Interventions for Learners who Struggle: ADHD, Learning Disabilities, Autism Spectrum Disorders and Oppositional or Non-Compliant Learners

Laura A. Riffel, Ph.D.

Jessica R. Eggleston, Ed.D.

www.behaviordoctor.org

www.twitter.com/behaviordoctor

www.blogtalkradio.com/behaviordoctor

caughtyoubeinggood@gmail.com

Copyright Page

ISBN 978-0-359-60267-4

This book is from Behavior Doctor Seminars ®™

www.behaviordoctor.org

Laura A. Riffel, Ph.D.

caughtyoubeinggood@gmail.com

This book was developed to be used in conjunction with a seminar on Learners who Struggle through Behavior Doctor Seminars

Strategies for Learners who Struggle

Positive Behavioral Interventions and Supports

If you are part of a school implementing Positive Behavioral Interventions and Supports (PBIS), then you know there are definitely processes for the tertiary level of PBIS. This book is geared to help you with the targeted group level of PBIS, specifically the issue of working with children who are struggling because of mild disabilities like ADHD, Learning Disabilities, Autism Spectrum (mild), or Oppositional or Defiant Behaviors.

What particularly drew me towards PBIS was the notion of looking at behavior differently. Instead of calling behavior the bad behavior or the problem behavior, we were told to call it the target behavior. On first glance, this does not sound like much of a difference; however, it is a huge mindset change. Instead of thinking "bad kid" or "problem kid" "where can we send this kid?" The new wording makes us think of the behavior as what we are targeting to get rid of and not the child. We love the child; it is just the behavior we would like to extinguish. Much better use of words.

Your first assignment: Do not go back to your school and tell people who say "bad behavior" or "problem behavior" they are wrong. Just repeat back to them, "So, the behavior you would like to target for change is _____ (label the behavior in measurable and observable terms)." What will happen is, the staff will pick up your words and start to use them without even realizing you have changed their mindset.

The other thing we like about PBIS is that it broadens the intervention from only one approach-reducing challenging behavior to encompassing multiple approaches-changing systems, altering environments, teaching replacement behaviors, and appreciating positive behavior when it occurs, (Sugai & Horner, 2005). We will learn to build multi-modal designs when we write our BIPs.

Typical Classroom Makeup

You do know what you will get in your classroom, unlike Forrest Gump's Box of chocolates:

Sensory Integration	16%
ADHD	10%
Other Health Impaired	2.2%
Speech and Language Impaired	20.5%
Specific Learning Disabilities	20%
Hard of Hearing	1.3%
Intellectual Disabilities	11.6%
Emotional Behavior Disorders	8.6%
	90.2% of your classroom

This is based on a classroom of 25 students and data from the most current sources: Center for Disease Control, LD online etc.

Behavior Doctor Seminars®™ 2019

Ten Rules of Behavior:

1. Behavior is learned and serves a specific purpose (Bandura)
2. Behavior is related to the context within which it occurs (Bambara & Knoster)
3. For every year a behavior has been in place, we need to expect one month of consistent and appropriate intervention to see a change (Lally et al.)
4. We can improve behavior by 80% just by pointing out what one person is doing correctly (Shores, Gunter, Jack)
5. We use positive behavior specific praise about 6.25% of the time (Haydon, et al.)
6. When we want compliance in our students we should whisper in their right ear (Tomassi & Marzoli)
7. All behavior has function and falls into two categories: To gain access to or to Escape from (Alberto & Troutman)
8. To Gain Access- see chart below
9. To Escape From- see chart below
10. Your reaction determines whether a behavior will occur again. We have to change our behavior (Alberto & Troutman).

First things first, we should probably define what we mean by the function of behavior. The function is the end result that maintains the behavior. It is the reason a behavior occurs in most cases. Function is divided into two main categories:

Functions of Behavior

To Gain	To Escape
Attention: • Peers • Adults Access to preferred items or environmental controls Sensory Integration (Input)	Work/Tasks/chores People • Adults • Peers (Think bullying) Pain • Emotional • Physical Sensory (Overload)

To Be A Real Intervention:

- It has to stop the behavior
- Be proactive not reactive
- Change the environment to address the Trigger
- Replace the Target Behavior with a New Behavior that is Taught
- Address the impacT by feeding the replacement behavior and extinguishing the target behavior
- It has to be delivered long enough, with consistency and fidelity

In order to see any behavior, change, we need to address the Triple T's. (Pages 84 & 85)

Trigger	**Target**	**impacT**
What set the behavior in motion? Could be a direct antecedent (something that happened right before) or could be a setting event (something that happened in the near distant past)	What is the behavior you would like to target for change?	What is the student gaining or escaping by engaging in this behavior?
Environmental Change/Cue	**Replacement Behavior**	**Response Feedback**
What can you do to set this student up for success? What cues can you set up in the environment to help the student remember the necessary behavior changes?	What replacement behaviors have you taught the student? This can be done through: • Modeling • Peer mentoring • Video modeling • Social Stories • Video self-modeling • Counseling	How can you change your own reaction, so you feed the replacement behavior with the desired impacT and extinguish the Target behavior by withholding the desired impacT?

Environmental Change: 🌐

Replacement Behavior: ★

Response Feedback: 🔓

Non-Medicated Interventions for ADHD

In 2007, there were 2.7 million children taking drugs for ADHD according to the CDC (2013). These are some of the typical stimulant drugs used to treat ADHD:

- Adderall (Adderall extended release)
- Concerta
- Dexedrine
- Focalin (Focalin extended release)
- Metadate
- Methylin
- Ritalin (SR and LA)
- Vyvanse
- Daytrana
- Quillivant (XR)

Non-stimulant Drugs Used

- Strattera
- Intuniv
- Kapvay

Other Drugs Used

- Antidepressants (Elavil, Norpramin, Pamelor, Tofranil etc.)
- Catapres, Duraclon, Nexiclon
- Tenex
- Wellbutrin

This list is from www.webmd.com (2013)

Why is it important to know which drugs a student is on? Because of the side effects possible with these medications:

- Stimulant medications can cause decreased appetites and weight loss, sleep problems, headaches, and nervousness.
- In some rare cases, the drugs can cause cardiovascular problems, exacerbate psychiatric conditions like depression, psychosis, or anxiety.

Why do I mention this at all? Because it tends to be everyone's first instinct to suggest putting the child on ADHD medication. We believe we should try all non-medicated interventions first before we jump to starting a child on a medication.

Statistics on ADHD from the CDC (2013)

Approximately 9.5% of children ages 4 through 17 have been diagnosed with ADHD as of 2007. This is 5.4 million children. The percentage of children with parent-reported ADHD increased by 22% between 2003 and 2007. In the years 1997-2006 ADHD rose 3% per year. Since then, ADHD has risen approximately 6% per year. Boys are more likely than girls to be diagnosed with ADHD. Boys (13.2%) and Girls (5.6%) meaning boys are much more likely to be diagnosed, especially with ADHD hyperactive. Boys receive medication 2.8 times more frequently than girls for their ADHD. Teen rates increase faster than

Behavior Doctor Seminars®™ 2019

young children for ADHD diagnosis. There is a wide variation from state to state with Nevada having only 5.6% of their population and North Carolina having 15.6% of their population.

Great Book on ADHD

The Gift of ADHD: How to Transform Your child's Problems into Strengths by Lara Honos-Webb, Ph.D.

ADHD Interventions

The ADHD test is available on http://www.youtube.com/watch?v=0CbrQp3MIwc

Anatomy of Boys and Girls

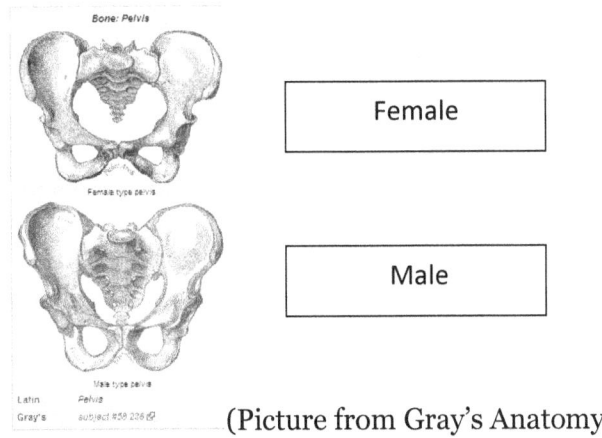

(Picture from Gray's Anatomy)

Proprioceptive Input

Proprioceptive input is knowing where your body is in time and space. Moving the body allows the learner to focus. Hard wood and plastic chairs restrict the normal movement required to provide this positive input. Changing how we seat students is of high importance to their overall learning.

Environmental Changes

Air filled cushions

- https://store.schoolspecialty.com/OA_HTML/ibeCCtpItmDspRte.jsp?minisite=10206&item=86918 (28.99)
- http://www.walmart.com/ip/Gold-s-Gym-25cm-Pilates-Mini-Ball/15580739 (Pilates Ball) (5.97)
- http://www.walmart.com/ip/Maha-Fitness-Balance-Disc-Trainer/19516929 (Pilates disk) (19.76)
- http://www.isokineticsinc.com/category/balanceproductsconsumer/product/ac35?gclid=CImp67jPlrgCFbTm7AodQxAAaw (13.00 (watch shipping)
- http://www.amazon.com/Inch-Balance-Exercise-Training-Stability/dp/B001KOD92Q/ref=sr_1_9?ie=UTF8&qid=1372967921&sr=8-9&keywords=pilates+core+disc (12.49- watch shipping)
- http://www.amazon.com/dp/B00AKKH5FS?psc=1 (12.97)

Other ideas:

- Sew the cushion into the chair using ½ yard of material
- Have two desks for the student
- Have a standing workstation (this is not a punishment)
- Send them on an errand
- Camping cushion
- Garden kneeling pad
- Stadium cushion
- Bath time relaxing pillow
- Kitchen cushion
- Use a token economy with the payoff being proprioceptive input
    - Using the teacher's chair (rollers and a little padding)
    - Sitting on a rocker glider stool
    - Sitting at the teacher's desk (big space to work)
    - Sitting at the work table in the room (science table or reading table)
    - Earning a fidget tool
    - Sitting in a rocking chair

Proprioceptive Input for the feet:
- Physical therapy banding between the two front legs of the chair
- Physical therapy banding kitty corner from back to front of desk legs
- Pantyhose leg stretched between two front chair legs
- Pantyhose with cut off piece of pool noodle run through the middle before tied to chair
- Allow students to take shoes off and wiggle toes- it reduces anxiety by 39%

Proprioceptive Input for fingers: (We call these fidget tools)
- Shag carpet for bath cut into small squares
- Artificial grass bathmat cut into small squares
- Dusting cloth
- Stress ball
- Bendable toy
- Putty, tacking, clay
- Koosh ball
- Velcro under the desk (one piece)
- Bathtub applique under the desk (textured anti-slip kind)

The BOINKS are from: https://www.fiddlefocus.com/

Bathtub appliques are from most dollar tree stores- Twelve for $1.00

Anchor Charts
Visual reminders in the room of appropriate behavior and appropriate social skills.

Acceptable Outlets. When a child has that 13th Mentos about to drop into the Diet Coke, we need to teach them how to calm themselves down. Fidgeting can increase retention of material by as much as 37%. Here are some ideas for acceptable fidget tools:

- Koosh ball keychain attached to desk or backpack
- Velcro attached under the desk
- Bathtub non-slip grip attached under the desk
- Pen chain (like the bank uses) attached to the bottom of the desk (no pen)
- Blue tacky that has been in the freezer
- Pompom ball from a craft store
- Beaded chain
- Fringe from sewing supplies
- Dust cloth
- Ribbon tied through button hole on a sweater
- Walk through any $1 store and you will find tons of soft objects that can be used for tools to help with attention through fidgeting

Auditory Cues. Download some 60-bpm music and make a folder of this music to play in your classroom. Have a song that you have recorded along with a ding that occurs every 30 minutes, one that dings every 45 minutes, and one that dings at 25 minutes out of 30 and so on. You decide what time frames you need. This helps the students who are good at auditory skills to tune into "time passing" and the five-minute warning for the time being almost up.

Heart rates. Students with aggressive behaviors tend to have a heart rate of 147 bpm on average just prior to the aggressive act (45-90 seconds prior). Children with impulsive and hyperactive behaviors will have higher heart rates as well.

The resting heart rate is 60 bpm. Music set around 60 bpm can have a calming effect in the classroom. Here are some places to figure out beats per minute:

www.tinyurl.com/tangerinebpm

www.beatunes.com

Web sites with information on 60 bpm and lists of songs:

http://walk.jog.fm/popular-workout-songs?bpm=60

http://www.shortlist.com/entertainment/music/scientists-discover-most-relaxing-tune-ever

http://mp3bear.com/?q=songs+around+60+bpm

Messy Writing. Some students have messy handwriting, or they get so frustrated with holding a pencil they break the pencil in two. We have found many students actually like to write and have neater handwriting when they use these little rocket shaped pens or pencils. They are thicker lead, so the lead doesn't break when they write. They have a little oil in the lead, so they don't make the dragging sound on the paper. They are still number two lead, so you don't have to replace it for standardized testing. They are comfortable and it makes it a smaller motor movement for their writing. These can be purchased at office supply stores and discount stores. We also purchase them in bulk from www.penagain.com – You can take a picture of them

 into your favorite discount store and tell them you would like to send parents there to get them and the manager will order them to have on hand. It's called the Twist N' Write Pencil.

NOTES:

Replacement Behavior: ★

Tools for Fidgeting:

While the tools themselves are an environmental change- the use of the tools is a replacement behavior taught to the student. Here are my expectations for tools. You can modify to suit your tastes:

Tools must:

- Stay with you
- Be one handed
- Be quiet
- Help you pay attention

If one type of tool doesn't work, have a secret signal that you use to help the student choose a different tool.

Video Modeling

Video modeling is a research-based strategy used for teaching generalized skills to a wide group (such as the entire classroom). Models are used in the video. This can focus on things like:

- Mindfulness
- Appropriate ways to pay attention in class
- Appropriate ways to ask a question
- Socially appropriate ways to fidget when uncomfortable

A great research article on video modeling is here:
https://eric.ed.gov/?q=video+modeling&pr=on&ff1=dtySince_2015&id=EJ1083458

Wynkoop, K. (2016) Watch This! A Guide to Implementing Video Modeling in the Classroom. *Intervention in School and Clinic*, v51 n3 p178-183

Fidget Tools (They call them toys- but I would stress that they are tools) -
https://www.youtube.com/watch?v=71PB_Rulk5M

Video Self-Modeling

Video self-modeling is a research-based strategy used for teaching specific skills to a single student or very small group. It is typically associated with learners with autism; however, we find it useful with neurotypical peers and any struggling learner. The Siskin Institute has a wonderful video explaining what it is and how to use it.
https://www.youtube.com/watch?v=nZv9sBtQbHE

Behavior Doctor Seminars®™ 2019

Here's an example of how to use Video Self-Modeling with teaching academic skills.

https://www.youtube.com/watch?v=aa4aV2OzjR4

Anchor Charts

Anchor charts can be placed in the room to give booster shots of socially appropriate ways to pay attention. While this is an environmental change in itself- the teaching of the behavior would be part of replacement behaviors.

Vibrating Watches.

(Again, this is partially environmental and partially a replacement behavior) Having a watch with a silent reminder to pay attention can be very helpful for those students who have ADHD inattentive or for children who appear to have become time blind. We have found these watches which were originally designed to remind children to go to the bathroom, are very helpful to remind students to come back to reality and pay attention. The watches can be set to vibrate at any interval the adults choose. It will vibrate for a few seconds and then reset itself for the next time segment. The student does not have to touch the watch to make it reset. Here are some we have found:

We did a search on Amazon and sorted the watches from least expensive to most:

http://www.amazon.com/gp/search/ref=sr_cb_?sf=sbc&rh=i%3Awatches%2Cn%3A377110011%2Ck%3Avibralite&sort=price&keywords=vibralite&ie=UTF8&qid=1373308108

Behavior Doctor Seminars®™ 2019

We made a tiny url- http://tinyurl.com/vibralitewatches . **This link should work.**

Social Groups.

Make PowerPoint social narratives to help the student learn how to join conversations and make friends. Go to www.behaviordoctor.org. Click on training and then material download. Scroll down to Relationship Narratives. This page is filled with sample relationship narratives to use with children who are having difficulty with social skills, transitions and targeted behaviors.

Organizational Skills

Many of our students struggle because they are disorganized. Here are some ideas to help organize the students. for this part of the book on page 78.

Color Coding.

I think educators should teach organizational skills to students at every age level. When I worked with incarcerated youth, I was amazed that they could lose an assignment in such a small space. I was only able to give them file folders, so I gave them a color folder for each subject.

- Red= Reading
- Orange= Language
- Yellow= Math
- Green= Science
- Blue= Social Studies
- Purple= Other

When I gave them a duplicated copy of work to complete, I would run a coordinating color marker down the side of the papers, so it had a tinge of that color on the edge. The students knew which folder it went in if they found a loose paper. If the students produced the work themselves on notebook paper, I taught them to take their crayon and make a dot in the upper right-hand corner. (We couldn't have markers because they would sniff them.)

When I moved to Kindergarten, I used the same color-coding system for them, and I had them keep their work in a plastic magazine stand beside their table. When I worked with older students, I had them keep their folders in a large 2-inch binder, so all their work was together. This color-coding system has worked well for me over the years. My turn-in bins matched the color of the work to be turned in as a cue for correct filing within the classroom. My bulletin boards even matched the color-coding system. Example: Anything having to do with Math was on a yellow bulletin board.

Parents.

When you have open house night, talk to parents about color coding their children at home. We used a color-coding system for our three children. Each child had a milk crate by the back door. At night, before they went to bed, they had to fill their milk crate with the proper materials to go to school the next day: backpacks, permission forms, PE shoes, Library books, science experiments etc. had to be ready to go before bedtime. This avoided any scuffling in the morning when children and adults tend to be tired and cranky.

Backpacks.

Get a luggage tag from the dollar store. Flip the address card over and write all the things that need to go inside the backpack from school to home and home to school. More cards can be cut and labeled "A" day, "B" day. Etc. The cards can be color coded to assist those students who need more mnemonic cues. This helps students be prepared. They can take an erasable marker and draw a line through each thing as they load the backpack.

Agenda Books.

Some students never get their assignments written down in the agenda book. Many times, this is not due to laziness. It is due to the inability to transfer from the vertical plane to the horizontal plane. This is a learning disability and educators would never mark a student down in grade for having a learning disability. For these students who habitually don't get the assignment written down, print off the assignment on an address label and teach the student to go get the label off your desk and put it in their agenda book. This is not "babying" a student. This is making an accommodation for their disability. Remember what your objective is- is it to teach writing and copying or to get the assignment done?

Maps.

For those students who can never find anything in their desk or locker. Make a map of what their desk or locker should look like (visual – kind of like the people who outline everything on their tool wall in the garage, so they know where it goes). Post it inside the locker or inside the desk and then have the desk or locker fairy visit from time to time and if the desk or locker is neat, the student earns a prize (new pencil or special chair for the day).

Executive Function Skills

Executive function is being able to think "How is this decision going to affect me?" Basically, it is being able to think ahead. Unfortunately, during the pruning years (teenage), this becomes a difficult task because the brain is so busy pruning the unused portions of the brain. How to think is basically what we are talking about in executive function.

We like to use Ned's Head (children's game) to talk to student about things that can be distractors to thinking. We got the idea for Ned's Head from Jill Kuzma on Pinterest. We liked it so much, we bought

one to use with students we were counseling. Using an inanimate object to talk about things that are going on helps students relate it to themselves.

These are things that distract me **inside** my head:

- Is my locker combination right-left-right?
- I wonder what we are having for lunch?
- I wonder if my brother will call tonight?
- I wonder what level I can get to on Minecraft tonight?
- Did I remember to feed the dog this morning?

Things that might distract me **outside** my head:
- Who has on that perfume? They took a bath in it.
- That tag in the back of my shirt is itching like crazy. I need to pull it off.
- Look at that hole in the teacher's shirt under her arm
- Who is tapping their pencil on the desk?
- I smell tacos- we must be having tacos for lunch.
- I can still taste that breakfast burrito- I need a drink of water

More Detail on executive function:
- Attention
- Cognitive activation
- Emotional control
- Flexibility
- Goal setting
- Inhibition
- Initiative
- Memory
- Organization
- Planning
- Problem solving
- Self-monitoring
- Shift
- Time management
- Working memory
    - From Moraine, P.; 2012 - Helping Students Take Control of Everyday Executive Functions: The Attention Fix- available through www.amazon.com

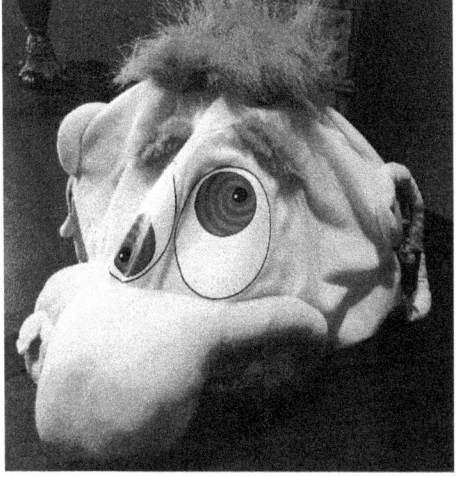

We can teach students ways to help with all of these topics.

Function	Techniques to Help
Attention	
• Internal	• Vibrating watch set for a predetermined time frame. Teach student that when the watch vibrates to check themselves and make sure their mind is on the task at hand. (vibralite3) • Secret cues between teacher and student to remind them to come back when it looks like Elvis has left the building • Teach students how to push the ideas that float in out of their head- recognizing a thought is a distraction and pushing it out as we focus on the correct thoughts
• external	• Vibrating watch set for a predetermined time frame. Teach student that when the watch vibrates to check themselves and make sure their mind is on the task at hand. (vibralite3) • Teach student to make a note of external items that cause them to be distracted and to discuss with teacher ways to avoid those items (hallway distractions, sitting by certain people, sitting near the window etc.) • Teach student how to use white noise to block out external distractions when they are working at home or even using headphones to listen to white noise when working on independent work. • Let them choose a seat that provides them with the best spot to pay attention •
Cognitive activation	• Some students think too much- when the teacher is presenting new information, instead of connecting it to prior learning their brain connects that with another thought and then another thought and then another thought, and they lose the connection with the current topic. • Give students time to illustrate or free-connect on the topic of the day • Have the students use self-recording data on best times of the day for alertness- schedule new material to be taught during this time of day • Let the student create and teach a lesson to the class • Pre-test the student with questions that might be on the test • Provide visual cues like concept maps that allow the student to illustrate similarities and differences- • Provider mnemonic reminders that cue them to attend to specific main ideas • Teach students how to collaborate with other students so they can actively converse on the topic with another person • Teach students how to expand key ideas of the lesson • Teach students how to scaffold their thinking from the bottom-up – start with details and build up to big picture- then big picture down to details – top-down • Teach students how to tell the difference between a main idea from a detail • Teach the students how to actively process information- like using a T chart for note taking and tying lecture to book and adding illustrations • Teach the students how to scan or skim to pull out the important information • Use a timer to make sure they do not get lost in the assignment • Use the students focused interest into what you are teaching. If the student likes dinosaurs, use information about dinosaurs to teach that day's math lesson

Emotional control	• Teach students how to override impulsive outbursts. It will be different for each student
	    o Yoga
	    o Calming breathing
	    o Stress balls

		<ul><li>Karate (training outside of school) helps with concentration and control</li><li>Walking</li><li>Positive self-talk</li></ul>
Flexibility		<ul><li>Model flexibility for the students. Show them how we use flexibility in our daily plans etc.</li><li>Teach students how to understand change is inevitable- PowerPoint social stories with change possibilities built into them.<ul><li>We will have reading and then spelling today<ul><li>But there could be a fire drill today<ul><li>That's okay because we will come back after the drill is over</li></ul></li></ul></li><li>We will have Library today<ul><li>But there could be a substitute teacher in library today<ul><li>That's okay, we'll still have Library</li></ul></li></ul></li></ul></li></ul>
Goal setting		<ul><li>Teach students how to set a long-term goal with short term objectives.</li><li>We really like a program from California called SWAG- students with a goal- it's a great workbook series and has helped a lot of students stay in school</li><li>Teach students how we set goals for ourselves and how we meet those goals</li></ul>
Inhibition		<ul><li>Self-consciousness can hinder learning in the classroom if a student is afraid of being called on</li><li>Figure out who is easily embarrassed and work out a secret cue with them, so you don't call on them when they aren't prepared. You will find that if you give them this courtesy, they will start to open up and share when they are ready. Otherwise, they will just shut down.</li></ul>
Initiative		<ul><li>Inventiveness- help students feel like they are explorers. This is how new businesses are born</li><li>Help them take ideas from one lesson and apply them to another.</li><li>Encourage resourcefulness and Ingenuity- it will be contagious</li></ul>
Memory		<ul><li>Mnemonics are handy tools to help with memory<ul><li>I used to teach students mnemonics to help them with spelling-</li><li>Their (has the word heir in it- it shows belonging) "Prince Charles is their heir to the throne." – There (has the word here in it- it is a place) "We are going here and there." They're (is missing a letter, it is a contraction meaning it is two words they and are.) They're going to the museum- or -They are going to the museum.</li></ul></li><li>Provide students with a simple clasp ring and 3 x 5 cards- write the things they need help memorizing on 3 x 5 cards and use these as a study guide</li><li>Help students figure out whether they are auditory learners or visual learners. (My daughter who is a combined learner would write her own flash cards, read the cards out loud as she recorded herself. Then she would lay in bed at night and listen to the recordings to help her memorize what she needed for each subject). (My youngest son, who is an auditory learner just had to sit in class and listen and he would know the material.) (I'm a visual learner. I can tell you exactly where information was on the page in the book because I visualize the words on the page.) Each person has a different learning style. Until we know how we learn best, we will fumble.</li><li>A good book *Teaching Secondary Students Through Their Individual Learning Styles*, Rita Stafford and Kenneth J. Dunn; Allyn and Bacon, 1993</li></ul>
Organization		<ul><li>We like having the students draw maps of what their lockers and desks should look like.</li><li>We like rewarding students with praise for having their lockers and desks look like their maps. We used to give out pencils for neat desks and neat lockers.</li></ul>

| | | • Teach students how to organize their notebook- We like to use color coding (see first Duct Tape Book)
• Teach students how to organize their day
• Teach students how to organize their homework plan
• Teach students how to organize their backpack- use a luggage tag to write on the things that need to go home and come back to school |
| --- | --- | --- |
| Planning | | • Planning how to do things is a skill that has to be taught.
• Jill Kuzma has a great planning sheet that can be shared with students:
   ○ https://jillkuzma.files.wordpress.com/2012/12/homework-planning-sheet.pdf
• This is the kind of visual planning tool that will help students stay on track and develop life-long skills
• The more we can give students this type of structure, the more we will be giving them life-long skills
• Teenagers whose brains are pruning have a difficult time with this planning without the learning tools |
| Problem solving | | • We feel the best way to teach problem solving skills to students is for us to tell students how we problem solve. This is not just how-to problem solve getting along with others, it is how to problem solve what to do if you leave your homework at home, or your pencil breaks in the middle of a test.
• This can be taught through social stories, writing activities, reading activities, and more.
• Furthermore, problem solving is how we acquire new knowledge
• Being able to connect past learning with new learning and generalize that to future learning.
   ○ A great article with ideas for our classrooms is here: https://www.teachervision.com/problem-solving/teaching-methods/48451.html |
| Self-monitoring | | • John Hattie found the number one intervention for improving academics and behavior was students monitoring their own progress (Hattie, J.; 2008)
• We have used 3 x 5 cards, rubber bands from one wrist to another, paper clips from one pocket to another, laminated card inside desk or notebook, and any other trick to help students monitor behaviors they are trying to change. We have set beeps to go off in the classroom, vibrating watches, and word cues or silent cues from the teacher to help them look at their behavior of the moment.
• This is taught through private time with the teacher and as much as possible no one else in the class should know what the student is measuring. Be careful not to label the card they are marking on with the behavior being measured. One of our adult friends told us the story of the speech teacher who drew a picture of a girl with her tongue hanging out and wrote, "Keep Your Tongue in Your Mouth" and laminated it and put it on her desk. All the kids read the card and made fun of her for years because of this. As an adult, it was obvious she was still clearly upset by the teasing that had occurred.
• http://www.interventioncentral.org/self_management_self_monitoring Here are some great ideas from intervention central. |
| Shift | | • We used to call this code-switching. Students have to be able to switch between tasks and also various steps within that task. These students are often referred to as students who have difficulty with transitions. This is why teenagers have such a hard time when all the teachers in the school do not have the same set of rules. They cannot switch of being able to chew gum in one classroom to not being able to chew gum in another classroom.
• It is not just students with autism who have trouble with this rigidity in thinking. |

	- Social stories are the best way to let younger students know about changes in routines, changes in steps to perform a problem, changes in how a work task will be completed. For older students, a simple visual schedule, or visualization of the steps will really be helpful. - A perfect example of difficulty with shifting occurs when children apply grammar rules to all words. Every child went through a phase of thinking things were "good", "gooder" or "goodest", instead of good, better or best. Eventually, most children learn that the rules do not apply all the time in language. We have to help them realize that shift happens in many situations.
Time management	- We all know adults who have difficulty with time management. We all know teachers who are still at school at 8:00 at night and most of the weekend. We can help future adults learn to be more cost efficient with their time by helping them set limits for themselves. - Helping students prioritize tasks and time - Helping students sense the passing of time- some students leave this planet and have no idea they were gone - Helping students create study routines and appropriate environments for studying - Helping students manage their papers and materials in a timely and organized manner.

Working memory	- There are two types of working memory: auditory memory and visual-spatial memory. It takes both skills to help students create a video recording of what is going on in their mind.
	  - Kids with executive function skills have a hard time holding onto the information that came in. They have less ability to use new information when doing independent work.
	- The teacher can "alert" the students to the importance of key facts and provide post-it notes for students to write down those key facts
	  - Easy strategy give each student a stack of post-it notes: every time the teacher shares a key fact that will be needed later, the teacher writes the word or idea on the board and draws a box around it. This alerts the students that they need to put this word or idea on their post-it notes.
	  - Students can have a special spiral notebook to keep their post-it notes in and use these when they are completing their independent work.

Executive Function Skills Are Not Just for Teenagers!

All levels should focus on teaching executive function skills. What can you do in your classroom to help your students be more on task?

Notes:

Response Feedback

Behavioral Techniques to Use:

Code Words. "I spy someone sitting up straight and tall and really paying attention." Privately code the student into the fact that when you say the word "SPY" you are really talking to them, but they will be the only one who knows this secret fact. When you say that in the classroom, look away from the student toward another group of students. Say, "You just earned the class a compliment on the compliment board." Go make a tally on the compliment board. There will be 8 children who think you were talking about them, plus you just improved the behavior of 80% of the class by labeling an appropriate behavior. A few minutes later when the student is doing what they are supposed to be doing, look right at them and smile and say, "I spy someone sitting up straight and tall and really paying attention. You just earned a compliment for the class." Then go make a tally on the board. This is good public relations for the student.

Secret Signals. Eat lunch with one student a day to get to know them better. When you have a student who is having difficulty, develop a secret signal to let them know they need to calm down using some of the techniques you have taught them. I always liked to use the Carol Burnett ear tug. I would use it if I wanted the student's attention and they would use it if they wanted my attention but didn't want to raise their hand and let everyone in the class know they needed help. Rick LaVoie tells of a secret signal where he tells the student he will only call on them if he is standing in front of them. This lets the student put all their energy into listening and learning and not worrying about whether or not they will get called on and be embarrassed because they didn't know the answer to a question.

Behavior Tips

Student Teacher Rating Sheet (this is actually a replacement behavior and response change technique) (Worksheets begin on page 68)

Laura Riffel's modified Check-in/Check-out (CICO) called the Student Teacher Rating Sheet is at the back of this book. Instead of using the PBIS model of 2-1-0 and the model of the teacher giving the student a score, this model uses 3-2-1 and the student and the teacher rate the student's behavior each hour and then try to match. The student earns points for matching the teacher. The student still takes this sheet to the CICO person at the beginning and end of the day; however, the parents are a key part of this program. The parents reward the student based on the number of points they earn each day. For an electronic version of this program: Go to www.behavordoctor.org- click training, material download, and then scroll to behavior intervention planning - it is called the Student Teacher Rating Sheet

- For a graphing tool to measure the points: Go to www.behavordoctor.org- forms and tools, and then scroll to data collection tools and look for graphing tool for Excel Spreadsheet for SBR

Secret Agent. Teacher has a cup with Popsicle sticks in it. Each stick has a student's name on it. The teacher draws up a stick in the morning and looks at it but doesn't show it to the students. The teacher gives a behavior he/she is looking for that day. If the student whose name was drawn follows that rule all day, that student will earn a prize for the whole class. The prize is something the teacher probably would have done anyway (but the students don't know that). For example, if you have a special art activity at the end of the day, don't tell the students ahead of time. Make the students think they earned it.

- At the end of the day if the secret agent student has not followed the rule, do not say, "Jamie did not follow the rules today, so there is no prize." You might as well say, "Boys and Girls, beat Jamie up on the way home tonight."
- At the end of the day, if the secret agent did not follow the rule, choose to say another student's name who did follow the rules. Have a private conversation with Jamie that sounds like this:
  - "Jamie, what if you had been the secret agent today? The whole class would have been counting on you. Tomorrow, let's try this again and I'll give you a secret signal to remind you to follow the expectation. Maybe I'll draw your name tomorrow." (Develop a secret signal between you and the student- like an ear tug (you tug on your ear- not theirs ☺)
- One of my schools uses this for line walkers. They choose a secret line walker each trip down the hallway. The secret agent earns 30 seconds of extra time at the end of the day to read or draw or have recess. By the end of the day, the students could earn up to 5 minutes of extra time. Teachers say the time saved by not having to get after the students is far greater than 5 minutes.

Social Autopsy. (This is actually an environmental change, replacement behavior, and response feedback technique all in one) Rick LaVoie coined the term "social autopsy" in the 1990's. It did not catch on then as well as it works now due to all the CSI shows. Every student knows what an autopsy is, and they are willing to do one on their behavior. The components are having the student write or draw the following:

1. Here's what was going on:
2. Here's what I did that caused a social error:
3. Here's what happened when I did that:
4. Here's what I should do to make things right:
5. Here's my plan for the next time I find myself in this situation:

The social autopsy is then laminated and put in a special folder. The student is reminded every day at the time of day they tend to engage in target behaviors to look at their planning folder. This works much better than a "think sheet". There is a blank social autopsy in the back of this book on page 80.

Information for YOU

Movie on Brain Structure. Thom Hartmann's video clips you might like to watch and ponder: http://www.youtube.com/watch?v=kJ-Px2OmCJw Are We Drugging Our Kids Into Stupidity? Also, this movie where Thom Hartmann interviews Dr. Richard Silverstein http://www.youtube.com/watch?v=kJ-Px2OmCJw Topography of the brain of children with ADHD.

I like sharing this with educators because it's really something to think about when everyone at the table is quick to suggest that medication is the answer. While we agree that some students perform better and seem to need medication; many students would do just as well with non-medicated interventions.

Notes:

In order to see any behavior, change, we need to address the Triple T's.

Trigger	Target	impacT
What set the behavior in motion? Could be a direct antecedent (something that happened right before) or could be a setting event (something that happened in the near distant past)	What is the behavior you would like to target for change?	What is the student gaining or escaping by engaging in this behavior?
Environmental Change/Cue	**Replacement Behavior**	**Response Feedback**
What can you do to set this student up for success? What cues can you set up in the environment to help the student remember the necessary behavior changes?	What replacement behaviors have you taught the student? This can be done through: • Modeling • Peer mentoring • Video modeling • Social Stories • Video self-modeling • Counseling	How can you change your own reaction, so you feed the replacement behavior with the desired impacT and extinguish the Target behavior by withholding the desired impacT?

Environmental Change: 🌐

Replacement Behavior: ★

Response Feedback: 🔓

Learning Disabilities

Learning disabilities is a general term for students who have normal to above normal intelligence, but struggle with some aspect of learning. This could be a reading disability, a calculation disability, a language processing disability, a writing disability, and many other specific learning disabilities which can affect a students' ability to learn without accommodations and modifications.

For Neuro-typical students, this is how much they remember from each of these activities:

Method Taught	Percent Retained
Lecture	5%
Reading	10%
Audiovisual	20%
Demonstration	30%
Discussion Group	50%
Practice by Doing	75%
Teach Others/ Immediate Use of Learning	90%

From the National Training Laboratories (Alexandria, VA 2012)

How Hard Can This Be? (Lavoie, R.) We highly recommend watching his **Frustration, Anxiety, and Tension** (F.A.T.) City videos which are available in pieces on www.youtube.com or through your media resource center at your school district.

http://teacher.scholastic.com/professional/specialneeds/howhard.htm

Dyslexia Screener:

37 common traits for dyslexia. If you answer "yes" to 10 or more of the questions, further screening and evaluation should occur.

http://www.dyslexia.com/about-dyslexia/signs-of-dyslexia/test-for-dyslexia-37-signs/

Davis, Ronald Dell. (1992) 37 Common Characteristics of Dyslexia. Retrieved July 1, 2016 from Davis Dyslexia Association International. Dyslexia the Gift website: http://www.dyslexia.com/?p=254.

Environmental Changes

Assignment idea: (This is an environmental change and a replacement behavior)
- Take a file folder and cut two slits in the top half dividing it into thirds
  - Teach the student to put the paper inside and open the top third and do that work
  - Then open the middle flap and close the top flap and do that work
  - Then open the final flap and close the middle flap and do that work

Lighting. The flickering of the fluorescent lights can be a distraction. Consider writing a grant to get funding and choose to put in www.huelight.net panels. The panels are about $20 apiece and all but stop the flicker from coming through. This is very helpful for eye strain, especially for our students with reading disabilities (scotopic sensitivity syndrome (SSS)). These students see the letters jumping up and down on the paper. As my friend who discovered she had this in her 50's said, "You don't know what you don't know." She thought everyone saw letters on text that way and wondered how they could read so much faster than she did.

- Use lamps around the room with incandescent light bulbs and leave overhead lights off
- Use natural light as much as possible

Article on the high numbers of prison inmates who have SSS: (FYI) on why it's important to catch it when the students are young:
https://eric.ed.gov/?q=scotopic+sensitivity+syndrome+&pr=on&ff1=dtySince_1997&id=EJ614098

Article on the use of colored overlays:
https://eric.ed.gov/?q=scotopic+sensitivity+syndrome+&pr=on&id=EJ414741

There has not been a lot of research on this topic, unfortunately. Both of these articles are quite old- but interesting.

More Writing Utensils that may be helpful to students struggling with dysgraphia:

For students who tend to get so frustrated they break their pencils:

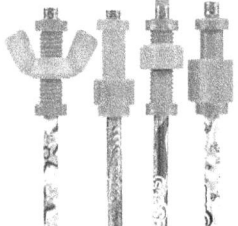

There is a company that makes totally bendable pencils. I cut them down into four pencils instead of one really long one. Oriental Trading Company sells them for $5.95 a dozen http://www.orientaltrading.com/neon-flexible-pencils-a2-5_968.fltr

For students who need to fidget while they think about their writing:

These are from http://www.amazon.com/Finger-Fidget-Pencils-Set-4/dp/B006RO3P96 $17.97 for four of them.

For students who nervously chew while thinking about their writing:

Use refrigerator tubing attached to the end of the pencil. It is non-toxic (this is the water line that brings water into the fridge) - cut off a two-inch section and attached to the end of the pencil. They can chew on the end of the pencil without ruining their teeth on the metal band. This tubing is about 49 cents a foot. It's food grade BPA free, so it's safe to use with students on their pencils.

Copying from the Board. For some students, it is very difficult to transfer what they see on a vertical plane to a horizontal plane. This is often an undiagnosed learning disability. An easy solution make 20 copies of what is on the board the first few days of school. Say to the students, "I know some of you might have trouble seeing the board because of the glare or where you are sitting. Here is a copy of what is on the board so you can copy it on your paper for your notes. I need these back to save for next year's students to save paper, so give these back when you are finished." After a few days, you will know who needs them and who doesn't and that is the number of copies you will need to make. For those students with dysgraphia, it might be best to take a picture of the board and email it to them. Remember your objective. Is your objective to learn how to write or to get the material down for study purposes?

Whole Brain Teaching. Students have target behaviors the most when the teacher is lecturing or there is down time in the classroom. Whole Brain Teaching (WBT) is a way to engage the students in learning. It is fun and all students are on task most of the time. WBT was invented by Dr. Chris Biffle. They have a website www.wholebrainteaching.com . Educators can earn staff development points for free by watching the training videos on this website. There are sample videos of teachers using the method at elementary, middle school, and high school levels. It is even used successfully at the college level.

Anxiety

Anxiety can side rail academic performance quickly, especially during high stakes testing. Here are some research-based ideas for reducing anxiety in the classroom.

Advanced Organizers. Advanced organizers help students organize their thoughts. Many times, teachers use KWL charts and flow charts for the whole class. Giving each student their own copy will help them cue into the important facts.

- Instead of plain K-W-L charts try these variations:
    - KWHL- What do you know? What do you want to know? How would you like to learn it? What did you Learn?
    - KWHLP- What do you know? What do you want to know? How would you like to learn it? What did you Learn? How would you like to prove it?
- Instead of plain flow charts, have the students make them on a PowerPoint in the computer lab and link each box to a movie or online link which will help them study. Have them email the PowerPoint to themselves at home for study.

Spelling. We know many adults who do not know how to spell. There was a period in education when teachers were told not to tell students how to spell a word. A lot of anxious kids freaked out when the teacher would not tell them the right way to spell a word. Some students cannot stand to make a mistake. We typically call them perfectionists. Many of us would fall into that category. Here are some ideas to help specifically with spelling:

- Mnemonics paired with Michenbaum's Five Step Cognitive Model.
    - On Friday, the teacher gives a pre-test on all the next week's spelling words. These are not graded for a grade, rather they are graded for what words received the most incorrect spelling variations.
    - The teacher then thinks up a mnemonic to help the students with those words.
        - For example: there, their, and they're
            - There is a place, we go here and there. It has the word here in it.
            - Their shows belonging. Prince Charles is their heir to the throne. It has the word heir in it.
            - They're is a contraction. It is shortcut word for two words, so it has an apostrophe in it.
        - On Monday, the teacher introduces all the words and shows the students how to write them using the new mnemonic.
        - On Tuesday, the teacher has the students perform the writing while he or she tells the mnemonic aid.
        - On Wednesday, the teacher has the students say and perform the writing while saying the mnemonic.
        - On Thursday, the teacher has the students whisper and perform the writing while whispering the mnemonic aid.
        - On Friday, the teacher has the students think it and perform the writing while thinking of the mnemonic aid.
            - Here's an example:
                - Monday. M-U-S-C-L-E-S (sung to the tune of N-E-S-T-L-E-S chocolate) – the teacher sings it as he or she writes it on the board about five times.
                - Tuesday. M-U-S-C-L-E-S (sung to the tune of N-E-S-T-L-E-S chocolate) – the teacher sings it as the students write it on their paper about five times.
                - Wednesday. M-U-S-C-L-E-S (sung to the tune of N-E-S-T-L-E-S chocolate) – the students sing it as they write it on their paper about five times.
                - Thursday. M-U-S-C-L-E-S (sung to the tune of N-E-S-T-L-E-S chocolate) – the students whisper it as they write it on their paper about five times.
                - Friday. M-U-S-C-L-E-S (sung to the tune of N-E-S-T-L-E-S chocolate) – the students think it as they write it on their paper for the spelling test.
- Magnets
    - For students who have a hard time writing, they can manipulate magnets to spell the word. We use this with children with autism who are just developing their skills. We take the letters of the word and put them in a baggie with a picture or plastic replica of the object they are spelling. We hand the baggie to the student and have them take out all the objects and manipulate the letters into the correct spelling.

- As the students gain expertise with this method, a foil letter can be added to the mix. In other words, for the word FISH- there would be a plastic fish and the letters: F-I-S-H-J
- **Sandpaper**
  - For some students, if they feel the letters as they write (tactile learners), it helps them commit the action to memory. Having the students write on sandpaper with a crayon will help them with the muscle memory for how to write the words.
- **Wikistiks** can be used in the same way. The student would then trace the letter with their finger after they formed the letters of the word.
  - Wikistiks can be used again and again and sandpaper is a onetime use product
- **Dictionaries**
  - We made a book for each student with an alphabet letter on the top of each page. As the students asked how to spell a word, we would write it on a 2 inch by 2 inch post-it note and give to them to put in their personal dictionary. The students were trained to look up their dictionary first to see if they had already asked how to spell the word.

Word Searches. Many teachers still use word searches. For students with visual discrimination issues, these can be quite daunting. Teach the student to use a ruler to find the words. They can move the ruler horizontally, vertically, and diagonally.

Kinesthetic Learners. Many students need to move to learn. A fun way to make it a movement game is to purchase a cheap plastic ball from a discount store. These balls are usually in a large bin in the toy department and cost around $3. With a permanent marker, divide the ball into sections and write a question or math problem in each section. Have the students sit or stand in a circle and toss the ball from one person to the next. Wherever the catcher's hands land, they read the question below their right thumb. They read the question out loud and then the student answers the question to earn points for the class. The class can be divided into teams who earn points. The student then passes the ball to someone who has not had the ball and the game continues until everyone has had a chance to partake. For Kindergarten students or students who do not know their right from their left, the teacher can paint a small amount of red fingernail polish on their right thumbnail and this will help them. By the time the polish wears off the student will know their right from their left. (Be sure to ask parents before you pain fingernails).

Multiplication Facts. If a student has difficulty with memorization of multiplication facts, a spatial approach is best. Use a number chart or matrix of the numerals 1-100 and have students county by "4"s and color in the box of every fourth number. Seeing the visual pattern helps man students who learn best visually and spatially. See page 70 for a blank number chart for you to use. Page 69 is a sample.

Have the students make a PowerPoint coloring in the boxes using tables and the fill-in tool. Have them make a page for 1's, 2's, 3's, 4's, 5's, 6's, 7's, 8's, 9's, 10's, 11's, and 12's. Then have them link to the Multiplication Rock music for each page and they can listen to the music and watch the page as they learn their multiplication facts.

Fun with Math

Some kids like to learn tricks that don't really help them that much- but they are fun to learn. I only mention them in this book because if we can make Math seem like a fun concept, perhaps the students will want to learn more: Here are a couple.

Sevens:

Take a box grid of 9 squares

Starting at the bottom of each row number the boxes backwards like this:

7	4	1
8	5	2
9	6	3

Now use this pattern:

0-1-2

2-3-4

4-5-6

(last number repeats in next row)

Fill in the boxes with these numbers

07	14	21
28	35	42
49	56	63

7x1=7, 7x2=14, 7x3=21, 7x4=28, 7x5=35, 7x6=42, 7x7=49, 7x8=56, and 7x9=63 Just for fun- won't really help them, but they'll have fun playing with it.

Nine Fingers

9 x 4 = 36 Hold down finger number "4". There are 3 fingers before it and 6 fingers after it- so the answer is 36.

3+6=9 is also a way to see the nine trick- all the answers equal nine

0+9+9
1+8=9
2+7=9
3+6=9
4+5=9
5+4=9
6+3=9
7+2=9
8+1=9
9+0=9

Once again, these are just fun facts and won't really help a child "learn" the facts.

Fun Ways to Learn (Ideas from Pinterest)

Nametags. Many teachers wear a sticker on their clothing to help students learn difficult facts. When a classroom is studying difficult facts, give each student a self-stick name tag with an important fact on it. This can be Math, or any other subject. From that point on for the day, have the students refer to each other as the fact on the name tag and not the student's real name. For instance, during class meeting instead of saying, "I'd like to compliment Susie for picking trash." A student could get the Koosh ball and say, "I'd like to compliment the capital of Kansas is Topeka, for picking up trash." It's funny and the students will remember the difficult facts.

Sandwich Board. Many teachers have worn aprons with specific facts on them. A lot of teachers now carry a small white board with them as they walk down the hallway, the teacher walks backwards with a fact on the board. If the students have to wait a few minutes to go into a special class, the teacher might write facts on the white board and have the students whisper the answers.

Floor. Turn your floor into a bulletin board. Write facts on the floor on clear contact paper, or solid color contact paper and stick it to the floor. Masking tape or duct tape works well too. It does leave a sticky residue on the floor, but "Goof-off" takes it right off. If your floor is carpeted, the stickiness will wear off with the students walking on the carpet.

Vocabulary. When teaching new vocabulary, make index cards. One card will have the word and one will have the definition. Pass out one card to each student. Have them find their other half. They will have to problem solve to figure out who has the word and who has the answer. They will have to go around and read the answers over and over again to learn who to pair up with in the classroom.

Go Fish. When students are learning new vocabulary or new facts, the board can be turned into a small memory game. Every time you catch the class being "good", choose a student from your stick jar to come up and try to match a pair. When all the pairs are matched, the class earns a prize. It's a win-win. The students are hearing facts and learning to use their brains to remember where something is on the board and they are working in a group contingency for a group payoff.

Sequence. When learning difficult sequences, give out index cards with the sequences on them. Let's say for some reason you were teaching the order of the presidents. Write each president's name on an index card. You might write the years they were president below their name. Pass out all the cards and then have George Washington start. The first student would say, "I have George Washington who was president from 1789 to 1797. Who has the second president of the United States?" The second student would say, "I have John Adams, He was the second president from 1797-1801. Who has the third president?" And, so on until the current president. This can later start some discussions about what was going on during each president's term.

- The same can be done with Math facts. "I have five. Who has five plus five?" "I have ten. Who has ten plus five?"
- "I have Delaware who became a state in 1787. Who has the second state to enter the union?" "I have Pennsylvania who became a state in 1787. Who has the third state to enter the union?"

Prefixes and Suffixes. Give each student two dice. The dice are blank dice you can purchase from teacher supply stores or you can use unifix cubes. On one dice, write the prefixes and suffixes you are studying. On the other dice write root words. Give each child a piece of paper between every two children. Have the students get in pairs and roll their dice to make new words. They are to write their new words on the paper if the word makes sense. They can check their new word in the dictionary.

Prefixes:

- Non
- Dis
- Re
- Pre

Suffixes:

- Able

- Ing
- Ous
- Er

Root Words:

- Descript
- Repair
- Port

Flip Books. Make students a flip book about themselves. Take sentence strips and leave one long and the rest half the size. Put the students name on the left-hand side and write "IS'. In other words, Charlie is……. The students will then write something about themselves on each card which is stapled to the right side of the long strip. Each page will form a sentence.

- Charlie is very tall.
- Charlie is very smart.
- Charlie is a lover of trains and planes.
- Charlie is not a lover of broccoli.

These can be fun to do during the first week of school and then share them during circle time. For older students, the sentences will be more complex, and the students can illustrate each strip.

Once the students understand this concept, they can make flip books for any subject you are studying. ………………………… would describe Japan. Each student can have their own topic and then they can be shared and passed to review for a test.

- ………………………………is an export of Japan.
- ………………………………is an import of Japan.
- ………………………………is the money unit of Japan.
- ………………………………is a large city in Japan.
- ………………………………is a major occupation in Japan.

Coded and Cued Assignments

Reading. For struggling readers, the letters can be color coded to help them determine long and short vowels for a short time. This will help them start to see the patterns in what makes a long vowel long and what makes a short vowel short. We used red for silent vowels, yellow for short vowels, and green for long vowels. Bossy "R" was purple (royal color…do what I say.)

Story problems. For some students understanding the words which mean subtract or divide and words which mean add or multiply are very confusing. Sometimes, we go through and circle the multiplication or addition story problems and put a square around the division or subtraction problems. Then we underline the words that tell them which made it that particular action.

The story of my life as a _____- grader. Give each student a roll of adding machine tape. Each day have the students write down something they learned that day.

They can write, draw a picture, use facts, or cut out a picture from a magazine if it works for what they learned that day. They begin rolling the tape the other way and use a paperclip to secure it. At the end of the year, they have a biography of what they learned that year. For young students, have them bring a shoebox from home which has been covered or spray painted a solid color. Make two slits in the box on the lid large enough for the tape to come up from the bottom and over the top and then down to the other side and down. Drill four holes, two on each long side of the box. Run a dowel rod through the holes from one side to the other. On the one on the left, run the dowel rod through the adding machine tape holding it in place. Run the adding machine tape up through the first slit in the lid and then back down through the second slit. Tape the end of the adding machine tape to the second dowel rod which has been run through from one end to the other. The students can then "roll" through their year and it will keep you from having runaway adding machine tape with little ones. Parents will love you for this because it will be a keepsake for their children. It will also be a nice "exit" ticket for the students each day.

Ways to Demonstrate Mastery Using Howard Gardner's Multiple Intelligences

After studying a subject, the students do not always have to take a paper and pencil test. They can show you they learned the material in a variety of ways. You will need to develop a rubric for each one based on the age level of the students you are working with and their particular intelligence level.

> **Linguistic.** These students are very good with words. They can write plays, movie scripts, puppet shows, television programs or develop crossword puzzles to demonstrate mastery. They will share with the entire class through their chosen medium.
>
> **Logical.** These students are very sequential and like patterns. They like multiple step science experiments. They might like to read two books and find the similarities between the two books. For instance, we had a student who found similarities between Abraham Lincoln and Ulysses S. Grant.
>
> **Bodily Kinesthetic.** These students like to touch and feel everything. They might like to build dioramas, create a dance representation of the events, or build an outside game based on the principles of what you studied. They can still write a report about the topic, but their main grade will be based on the bodily kinesthetic project.
>
> **Spatial.** These students are good with space and visualization. Let them draw, paint, or sculpt a product to depict what they've learned. Let them create the Battle of Gettysburg with Legos etc. They can create a maze game that uses flash cards with questions. These are the students that can look at those pictures of gears and tell you which peg will move when the gear goes left.
>
> **Musical**. These are typically your auditory learners. Let these students tell stories, write songs, or tell a story through interpretive drumming. These are the students that can tell you verbatim what you said on Tuesday at 9:17 a.m.
>
> **Interpersonal.** Let these students teach a lesson they develop for the class. These are the students that would love the challenge of a PowerPoint story to teach to the class. A lot of teachers rank high in this category.

Intrapersonal. These are the students who are shy, so they won't want to stand up in front of the class and give a lecture on the trials and tribulations of the depression era as it relates to the octogenarians who hoard money in the current century. These are the students who would be happy to take the multiple-choice test. However, these are also the very students who are self-motivated and could self-direct their own learning if given the opportunity.

Naturalist. These are the students who can draw upon certain features of the environment. Depending on the topic being explored in the classroom, there may be ways to connect this for evaluation. For instance, if you were studying the environment, these students might develop a science experiment for the class outdoors and bury the following in a pair of pantyhose: a Styrofoam cup, an empty soda can, a banana peel, some coffee grounds and a piece of paper. The student could bury this in the outdoor area of the school and then dig it up and comparing it to the original map of the pantyhose to show the class how things disintegrate over time.

Student Success. John Hattie, the author of Visible Learning: A Synthesis of 800+ Meta-Analyses Relating to Achievement found that students measuring their own success had a profound impact on their learning. Each student should have a notebook or folder for each subject. In the front of that binder, they should have a workbook sheet where they graph their score for each paper they turn in to the teacher and receive back. There should be no excuse for a child not knowing how they were doing in each class. See the example of a student scoring guide in the Workbook section for this part of the book on page 61.

Mathalicious. Mathalicious is a website filled with math lessons all linked to the common core and by grade level. The lessons are downloadable and all ready for educators to use. The user can set their own price for downloads and a few of the lessons are free for everyone to try. Mathalicious incorporates music, video, and interesting topics to teach the students a math lesson that will stick with them for life.

Games. Reality is Broken by Jane McGonigal is a book about why so many people (adults and kids) are addicted to online games. She suggests the best way to hook students in the classroom is to engage them in more game like activities. There are so many ways to do this:

1) Game templates. Turning any lesson into games like "Who Wants to Be A Millionaire?" or "Are YOU Smarter Than a Fifth Grader?" will entice the students to stay involved in the classroom activities. Go to www.behaviordoctor.org. Click on materials. Scroll down to games. This is a page with links to prepared game templates. All you will have to do is plug in your questions and answers.
2) Mouse Mischief:
    a. http://www.microsoft.com/multipoint/mouse-mischief/en-us/default.aspx
    b. Program allows educator to use PowerPoint and wireless mice to allow students to answer questions, answer polls, manipulate objects etc. Very fun and engaging and most schools have the correct wireless mice available in their computer lab. This is much cheaper than remote clickers for the class.
3) Thirty-Four ideas for using smartphones in the classroom
    a. http://www.teachthought.com/technology/36-smart-ideas-for-using-smartphones-in-the-classroom/
    b. Best ideas:
        i. Take a picture of the homework assignment or teacher produced work

        ii. Students videotape teacher's lecture for use during homework or test study
       iii. Students use agenda and email assignment to themselves
       iv. Use reality apps like planet finder or junaio in the class or on field trips
        v. Use as clickers for the Smartboard- ability to take polls etc.

4) Old fashioned games to make learning fun
    a. http://www.teachhub.com/engaging-classroom-games-all-grades
    b. Bingo, Bunco, Scrabble, Memory etc.

Notes:

Replacement Behavior Teaching

Kansas Learning Strategies. Kansas Learning Strategies is now called http://www.ku-crl.org/sim/ Strategic Instruction Model (SIM). They have developed a really wonderful training series that helps students who struggle with writing and reading. Here is one idea from them:

- **Mnemonics to help kids:**
- **PIRATES** for test-taking etc. This link gives proper credit to the authors- http://www.edgartownschool.org/uploads/files/nedine_cunningham/pirates.pdf
- Brochure on all the strategies: http://www.ku-crl.org/sim/brochures/LSoverview.pdf

Writing Strategy. 3-2-8 Paragraph (We learned about this from a teacher in North Carolina in 1987). First sentence has 3 ideas in it. Each one of those three ideas get two sentences. The eighth sentences wrap it up and restates the first sentence in a summarization.

- **Example:**

For my dog TJ's 14th birthday she went to ***Fleabuck's*[1]**, **Boneanza** [2], and **Barkin' Robbins Ice Cream** [3]. *At Fleabuck's she had a nice bowl of iced water. She asked for a sprig of mint in her water and splashed the mint, so she had minty fresh breath.* [1] We then trotted over to Boneanza for a nice juicy T-bone steak. TJ loves to gnaw the bone, so she quickly ate the steak and took the bone home in a "doggie" bag. [2] We then went to Barkin' Robbins for some ice cream as a birthday treat. TJ chose Backyard Bones Bubble Yum triple dip ice cream in a cup for her birthday dessert. [3] TJ's fourteenth birthday was a real treat at Fleabucks, Boneanza, and Barkin' Robbins.

I've used 3-2-8 with high school students and I've used it in Kindergarten with parent volunteers who served as secretaries as the students dictated the stories to them once a week.

Affirmations.

Students with learning difficulties will frequently struggle with self-esteem issues. One of the things we do each week is give the students a stack of 10 post-it notes and a printed sheet of positive affirmations for students.
https://theaffirmationspot.wordpress.com/2012/01/30/student-and-learning-affirmations/

The students choose 10 affirmations they like. They are taught to take these home and put them on their bathroom mirror or their closet door and make sure they read them before they come to school and again before they go to bed. We talk to them about the importance of the tape playing in their head.

Response Change

Three Stars and a Wish. By John Morris in Haversham, England (Ardleigh Green Junior School). Teachers were spending hours grading papers, circling everything that was wrong with a paper. Students were flipping the paper over to see the grade and then filing it in file 13. No learning is occurring. John had his teachers change the way they graded papers. No more one and done assignments:

- Teacher writes three things that are good about the paper
- Teacher writes one thing she wishes the student would work on to improve the paper
- Student rewrites the paper and then turns it in again for the same process.

Three Stars and a Wish Purple Edition. By Monika Marcel in Houma, LA

- Same idea- but it is graded by the purple paper eater (pretend monster). She grades it in a purple pen for her three stars and a wish and then slimes the edge with a little purple glitter eye shadow. The kids can't wait for the Purple Paper Eater to grade their papers.

There is a journal page to use the same philosophy in the workbook section on page 81.

Overwhelmed

Sometimes, you will have a student with special needs in your class and they will become overwhelmed due to noise, activities, difficulty etc. You cannot always get to them right away when they become overwhelmed. Have a plastic shoe box filled with educational games, headphones, stress balls etc. and keep it close to the child who becomes easily frustrated. Teach them when they get frustrated to go get the box and open it and use what is inside. This will be your cue to go over and get them on track as soon as you are finished with what you are doing. Better to have a child off task for a few minutes than have a child have a temper tantrum because they became overwhelmed and did not know what else to do. We like to use a box with a bright red lid because we will notice it moving in the classroom.

Four P's for Raising Self-Esteem

- Public Relations
- Proficiency
- Power
- Philanthropy

There is a worksheet at the back of this book. We have implemented the Four P's of Raising Self-Esteem with over 1000 students in Kansas and Oklahoma and have yet to find a student who did not respond. Our baseline was based on two factors: student grades and target behavior. We wanted grades to go up and target behaviors to go down. We implemented the Four P's for one month and measured grades and target behaviors again. In each case, there was a positive change in one or both of these factors. The key is consistency of implementing all four quadrants of the Four P's. (Worksheet on page 83)

Here is a PowerPoint on the Four P's- http://behaviordoctor.org/materialdownload/PowerPoints/4Psofselfesteem.ppt We have used this with over 1000 students and 100% have decreased one behavior and increased academics or attitude toward academics.

Adapted Books.

We were once called in to help with a blind student who was having behavioral issues in the regular classroom. He was very young and his biggest time for problem behaviors was in circle time when the teacher was reading aloud from a book. Imagine being blind and not being able to see the pictures to understand what was being read to you. No wonder he was rolling all over the floor to entertain himself. We got a list of the books the teacher might read and took the books and did the following:

- We outlined the shapes with puff paint.
- We put a small piece of foam between the pages so the pages would open easily from one to the next.
- We glittered some areas and put texture on things with the puff paint.
- If the class was reading about a frog, we got him a rubber frog to hold so he knew what they were talking about.

The point is, if a behavior is occurring, look at the situation from the child's point of view. What might be causing the behavior to show up?

In order to see any behavior, change, we need to address the Triple T's.

Trigger	Target	impacT
What set the behavior in motion? Could be a direct antecedent (something that happened right before) or could be a setting event (something that happened in the near distant past)	What is the behavior you would like to target for change?	What is the student gaining or escaping by engaging in this behavior?
Environmental Change/Cue	**Replacement Behavior**	**Response Feedback**
What can you do to set this student up for success? What cues can you set up in the environment to help the student remember the necessary behavior changes?	What replacement behaviors have you taught the student? This can be done through: • Modeling • Peer mentoring • Video modeling • Social Stories • Video self-modeling • Counseling	How can you change your own reaction, so you feed the replacement behavior with the desired impacT and extinguish the Target behavior by withholding the desired impacT?

Environmental Change: 🌐

Replacement Behavior: ★

Response Feedback: 🔓

Behavior Doctor Seminars®™ 2019

Students with Oppositional or Non-Compliant Behavior

Oppositional Defiant Disorder (ODD) is a tenacious pattern of behavioral outbursts that are angry or manifest as irritable or argumentative moods. These students are defiant toward parents, teachers, and other authority figures. They can display vindictive behaviors toward adults and peers. Sometimes these behaviors are specific to one location or context, other times it is a persistent demeanor that occurs in all settings. In order to be diagnosed with ODD, the intensity and frequency of these behaviors must be above and beyond the average range for a child's gender, culture, and developmental level.

These students lose their temper quickly. They tend to think rules are for other people. Frequently they blame other people for their own mistakes or target behavior. They tend to have a very short fuse with others and habitually annoy others. These students are impulsive beyond the norm for their age range. Their answer to many questions is instantly "NO". In other words, before they even know if something will be interesting, they will tell you they do not want to do it. We have met children in preschool who have these symptoms; however, most of the time it becomes apparent as children age through upper elementary and middle school.

What makes these students different from other students must be taken into account. The diagnosis manual dictates that for children under five years of age, the behaviors should occur on most days and last for at least six months. For children over five years of age, the behaviors should exist at least once a week for at least six months. The problem with these behaviors and students is that the behaviors most frequently occur in familiar settings. Visits to therapists and psychiatrists typically do not yield the same results witnessed at school and home. For this reason, data with anecdotal notes is highly recommended.

Many educators assume there are medications to assist with ODD symptoms. The best antidote is behavioral therapy as there are no medications indicated for ODD; however, many students with ODD also have co-existing conditions such as ADHD. Pharmacological choices may decrease some ODD behaviors when being treated for the co-occurring conditions. Students with ODD may also suffer from depression and anxiety which medication is indicated. It is important to help these students learn to self-regulate while they are young. It takes a concerted effort between home, school, and therapists to help these students be successful.

Environmental Changes

Heart rates

Playing music to slow the heart rate down can help everyone in the room remain cool, calm, and relaxed. Play this music at conversation rate, so the students can hear you talk over the background music. Students with aggressive behaviors tend to have a heart rate of 147 bpm on average just prior to the aggressive act (45-90 seconds prior) (Freeman et al., 2001). The resting heart rate is 60 bpm. Music set around 60 bpm can have a calming effect in the classroom. Here are some places to figure out beats per minute:

www.tinyurl.com/tangerinebpm (Free for ten uses- after that it is for pay)- you can take a snip shot of your iTunes account, so you know the beats per minute and then create your own playlist for the classroom.

www.beatunes.com – (This one is now $35- depends on how much you would use it for other areas of your life.)

Websites with information on 60 bpm and lists of songs:

http://walk.jog.fm/popular-workout-songs?bpm=60

http://www.shortlist.com/entertainment/music/scientists-discover-most-relaxing-tune-ever

http://mp3bear.com/?q=songs+around+60+bpm

Main Message: **Build a Relationship with the Student First- Discipline Without a Relationship Leads to Rebellion**

Nature Pictures

The University of Chicago found that looking at nature pictures reduced anxiety. Be sure to place some beautiful nature pictures in your room and seat your student with ODD where those pictures are in their line of sight. Playing nature pictures as the students enter the room in a slide show will also produce a calming effect for the students.

Feng Shui for Your Classroom

Bulletin Boards

Our students with ODD are influenced by many factors. One of those factors is the environment and pace of the classroom. If you have a student who is very non-compliant, resistant to authority, or truly ODD it will be important for you to make sure you have a calming environment. Many businesses use Feng Shui to increase productivity. In a sense that is what we are trying to produce in our classrooms. Based on her book, Feng Shui for the Classroom, Heiss (2004) tells us how to set up our rooms for optimum effect.

Using the components of Feng Shui in the classroom your room should have the following colors in the following places: (See the diagram). Businesses spend big money having designers come in and implement the practices of Feng Shui in their place of business to increase productivity, increase sales, and create harmony in the workplace. While you may not think you are selling anything, in reality you are selling the idea of becoming a life-long learner. Anything we do to make the environment conducive to life-long learning and loving learning is a step in the right direction.

Purple bulletin board • Clinic or Spa area • Posters of nature • 60 bpm music • Relaxation posters • Water feature • Blue bean bag	Red bulletin board • Battery operated candle • Gotcha tallies • Social information	Pink bulletin board • Team points • Team divisions if using whole brain teaching
Green bulletin board • Round wooden table • Student pictures	Yellow rug	White bulletin board • White round table • White metal clock • Extended learning
Blue bulletin board • Pictures of heroes Based on the work of Heiss (2004)	Doorway should be navy • Pictures of class • Pictures of you outside school	Gray bulletin board • Silver box • Wind chime • Globe

Feng Shui: Explanation of each area:

- Purple (This is your "hokey pokey" clinic "Where you turn yourself around.")
  - Clinic or Spa area- Don't think of this as a "time-out" corner – but a place to get your thoughts together. Students will use it on their own without disrupting the class if you set it up this way.
  - Posters of nature- Pictures of nature are anxiety reducing and most students who are upset are anxious about something.
  - 60 bpm music- The resting heart rate is 60 bpm and yet we find students who are aggressive tend to have heart rates that range in the average of 147 bpm. Music therapy suggests our hearts will match the music we are listening to. Play 60 bpm in this area or have a headphone and music available for students to listen to while getting themselves turned around.
  - Relaxation posters- Have posters about breathing back in this area. For example, a simple breathing technique like putting your tongue behind your two front teeth, closing your mouth and breathing in for a four count and out for a four count through your nose. If repeated 10 times it will slow your breathing down. Another technique for reducing an obsessive thought is to put your five fingers on your forehead and lifting each one up and back down two times. As you do this look up toward each finger. This action will help erase the obsessive thought.
  - Water feature- Running water is calming. A small fountain plugged in near this area will help students relax and get their thoughts together so they can come back to the area cool, calm and collected.
  - Blue bean bag- Your blue bean bag should be made of pleather for several reasons: 1) it's a cool material and 2) it's less likely to absorb critters of the lice variety. When students are upset, they tend to get hot, sitting into the cool

- bean bag will help cool them down, it's a nice sensory hug without touching someone.
- Red Bulletin Board
  - Battery operated candle- Candles make places seem homey. Since the fire marshal frowns on real candles, a battery operated one will work.
  - Gotcha tallies- This is important information. In your school, the teachers will be giving out "gotchas" if you are a (school-wide positive behavioral interventions and supports (PBIS) school and it is nice to keep a tally of how many tallies have been received by the room or the hour. Do not post individual names with tallies aside them because this would cause hurt feelings. Keep those tallies private and let other teachers know when a student has not received a tally for a while so they can catch them being good. If you are not a PBIS school, this can be where you keep your compliment board. We will discuss compliment board in the group contingency-group reward area below.
  - Social information- This is where you should post information about upcoming events that might be of interest to parents and students, the lunch calendar, and school vacation information etc.
- Pink bulletin board- This does not have to be a bulletin board. It can be a piece of pink tag board that is laminated. This area is for your group vs. group contingency. We will describe that in the contingency reward section below under group vs. group contingency.
  - Team points- You might have your class divided into the North vs. the South if you are a history teacher, or the peanut butters and the jellies if you are a kindergarten teacher. You might also have four groups instead of two based on how the students are grouped in cooperative grouping situations.
  - Team divisions if using whole brain teaching- Label the teams in this area and who is on what team. If you are a secondary teacher, you can even have the teams be Hour One, Hour Two, and Hour Three and so on.
- Green bulletin board- This does not have to be a bulletin board either- you can use a green piece of tag board which is laminated. Ask students to bring in pictures of themselves to put up in the room. This gives it a homey feel and makes the students feel like they are part of a family.
  - Round wooden table- This round table will be where you meet with students to discuss work or help with individual needs.
  - Student pictures- Send out a post card asking students to bring a picture of themselves when they come to "Sneak a Peak" night to put up on the bulletin board. This is a nice way to introduce yourself to them and as you put their picture up that night, you will get to meet them and their parents.
- Yellow- In the center of the room, you will put a yellow rug. This will be where you will stand so your podium or presentation table will be on this yellow rug.
- White bulletin board- This is where you will put a white round table, a white round clock, and your extended learning activities.
  - If you don't have room for a white round table near this area, you can use a white lazy susan on a shelf and put extended learning activities on the lazy susan.
- Blue bulletin board- This should be inside your doorway to the left. This is where you will put pictures of heroes and inspiring quotes.
- Navy doorway- The doorway should be navy. This can be a door covered with navy bulletin board paper or a navy poster on the door.

Behavior Doctor Seminars®™ 2019

- Put pictures of yourself outside of school engaging in your favorite activities (horseback riding, walking your dogs, picnic with your family etc.)
- Put pictures of your students from inside the classroom.
• Gray bulletin board- This should be inside your classroom to the right. You should have a silver box, windchimes, and a globe in this area.
    - We used the silver box for students to put important notes to the teacher. It can be as simple as a Kleenex box covered in tin foil.
    - The windchimes should be hanging from the ceiling and the globe should be sitting on a shelf in this area.

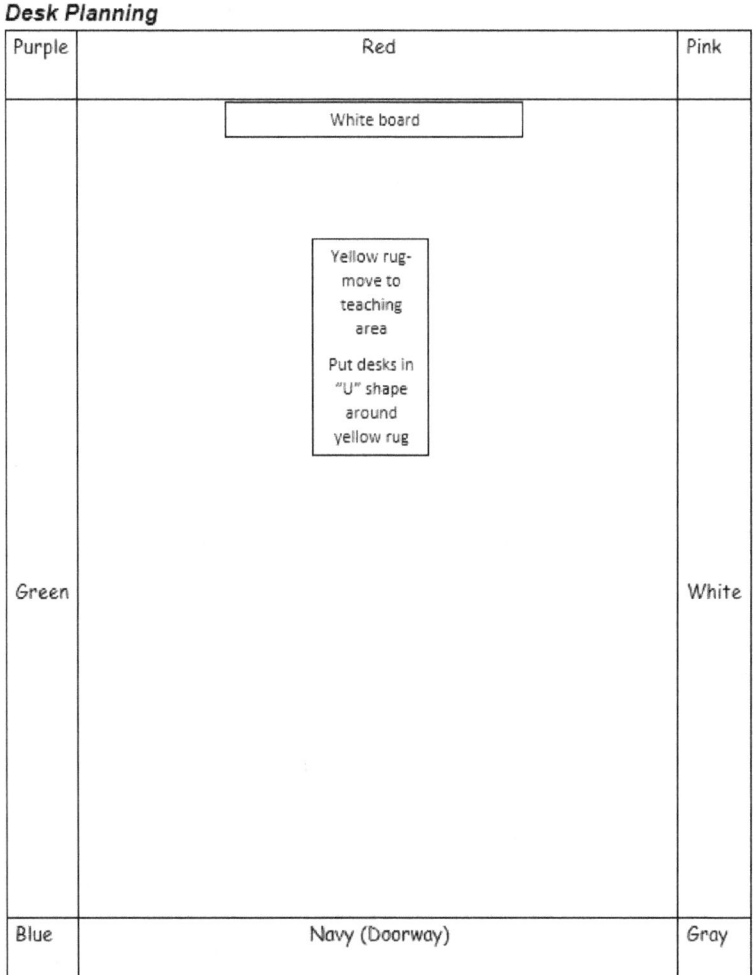

The bulletin boards only take up wall space. You will turn the diagram to match where your door is located for entry. The rest of the room should be designed for easy flow for the students and you. We like senatorial seating because the teacher is no more than two steps from any student when standing on the yellow rug in the center of the room.

Heiss, R. (2004); Feng Shui for the Classroom, Chicago, Zephyr Press

Calm Down Area in the Room

In your room, you should have a calming area. This does not need to look like a detention center. I would model how to use it. Pretend you are frustrated with your computer. Tell the students that you need a moment to get yourself together because this is troubling you. Go over to the area and have a seat and take some deep breaths. Count to ten. Whatever you do to calm yourself down. Then bring all your students over to the area and discuss how to use it. You pretending you are upset with your technology will be a great anticipatory set to your teaching how to use the calming area.

Show the students that in this area there are the following items:

- A blue pleather bean bag (I like blue because it is a calming color. I like pleather because it is less likely to harbor critters and it absorbs the coolness of the floor)
- A set of earphones hooked up to a music source with 60bpm music
- Calming pictures to look at
- Calming tools that can be held to destress
- Poster for how to calm down using breathing

You will change the explanation to match the age of the students that you are working. The main message is that all of us need to calm down at times and we need to find socially appropriate ways to do that.

In the calming area

You can do the following:

- Listen to the headphones of 60bpm music
- Practice Your Breathing
    - Tongue behind two front teeth
    - Close mouth
    - Breathe in through your nose to the count of four
    - Breathe out through your nose to the count of four
    - Repeat 10 times
- Use the stress tools to help you destress
- Look at the nature pictures
- Return to your seat when you have self-regulated.

Notes:

Replacement Behavior

Staying in Frontal Cortex:

The trip to BS (Brain Stem). We know what happens when we don't give our stomach what it needs or too much of something. We have to think about the brain as well. It needs water, stimulation, and oxygen. When we get upset, we tend to breathe through our mouth. Oxygen goes right into the lungs where it is needed the most; however, it starves the brain of oxygen and the only thing we have left to work with is our brain stem. A brain stem is all a lizard has in its head. When a lizard is confronted, it only knows how to do two things: fight or run away. What happens to you when you fight? What happens to you when you run away? Using the breathing technique will help you stay in prefrontal cortex where the synapses are firing in the front part of the brain. This will help you use your thinking skills to self-regulate your emotions.

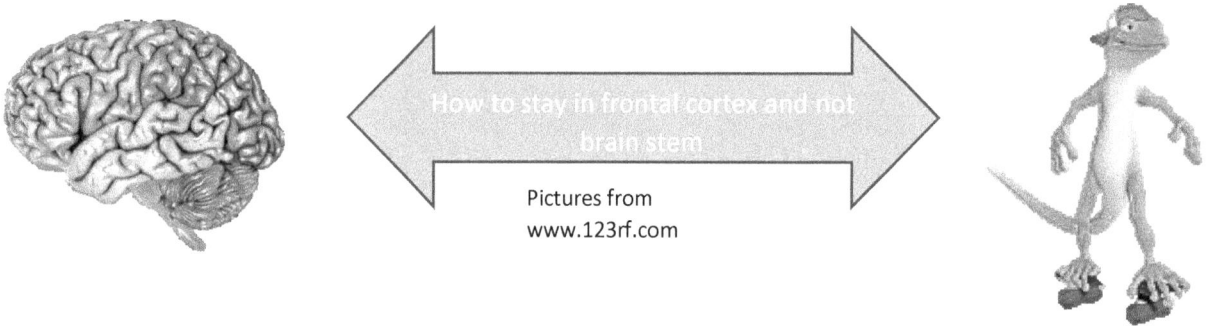

Pictures from www.123rf.com

I use my fist to show them the brain. I illustrate the brain stem with my thumb. Then I fold the other four fingers over the thumb and show them firing on all cylinders. This helps them remember the brain stem and prefrontal cortex.

Here is the video that I demonstrate in the training:
https://www.youtube.com/watch?v=RVA2N6tX2cg

It's called Just Breathe.

Breathing Technique. We teach students how to self-regulate using breathing techniques. The one student seem to like the best is this one:

1. Put your tongue behind your two front teeth
2. Close your mouth
3. Breathe in through your nose to the count of four
4. Breathe out through your nose to the count of four
5. Repeat this process 10 times.

To see Blake's Video Self-Modeling enactment of the breathing technique- go to www.behaviordoctor.org – under materials- click Video Self-Modeling. Blake is there.

Here is Blake's Power Card:

Front of card

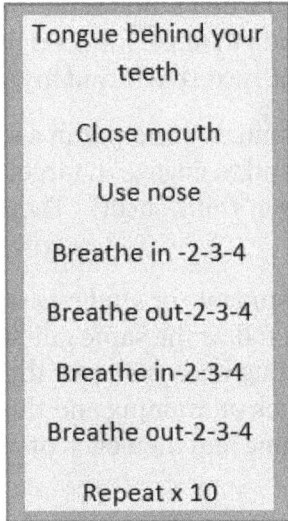
back of card

To see a different version of a Power Card Read the I Strategy in the next section.

Teach the "I" strategy for Independence

    Share the emotion (feeling)

    Explain the why (the cause)

    Make a request (the solution)

I feel frustrated when I don't know the answer, I need help.

We use these Power Cards printed through www.vistaprint.com

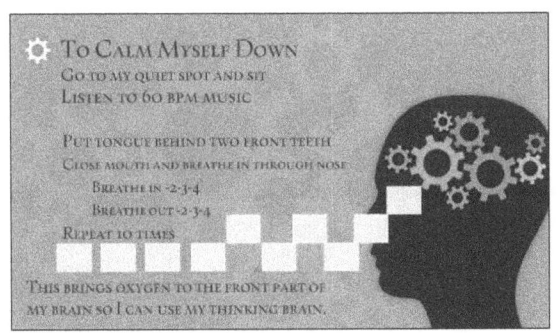 

Social Autopsy. Rick LaVoie coined the term "social autopsy" in the 1990's. It did not catch on then as well as it works now due to all the CSI shows. Every student knows what an autopsy is, and they are willing to do one on their behavior. The components are having the student write or draw the following:

1. Here's what was going on:
2. Here's what I did that caused a social error:
3. Here's what happened when I did that:
4. Here's what I should do to make things right:
5. Here's my plan for the next time I find myself in this situation:

The social autopsy is then laminated and put in a special folder. The student is reminded every day at the time of day they tend to engage in target behaviors to look at their planning folder. This works much better than a "think sheet". There is a blank social autopsy in the back of this book.

PowerPoint. For younger students or students with low verbal skills, a PowerPoint social autopsy works better. It will follow the same guidelines; however, the PowerPoint will have pictures of the student engaging in each step of the process. There is a sample on Go to www.behaviordoctor.org. Click on training and then material download. Scroll down to Behavior Intervention Planning and then click on the PowerPoint for Social Autopsy Sample.

Voice Level

Many times, teachers are heard saying, "Use your inside voice." Depending on your home, your inside voice level might be much louder than what the teacher is intending. Consider a child who lives in a home with 5 other children, they must talk louder to be heard. Consider a child who attends a daycare with 50 other children versus a child who attends a babysitter with six other children. Voice levels will be different depending on the context.

Use inches:

Pass out a ruler to each student. Have them practice in pairs talking in a 12-inch voice, 6-inch voice, 3-inch voice, and zero-inch voice. Use this philosophy on the bus and in the cafetoriums.

Sticks and Stones. Children with Oppositional Defiant Disorder need to learn bonding strategies in order to build relationships: Teach the ODD child to respond to others rather than react to others.

Technique for Kids. Cooking Spray- Be "PAM" -USE PAM on Your SPAM

Don't let words from other students stick to you. Be:

Proactive not reactive

Affirmative

Move Away

Proactive not reactive

Teach the child to have a plan to keep themselves in frontal cortex:

Teach them breathing techniques

Give them an outlet for tensing muscles such as a stress ball they keep in their pocket

Teach them how to go to their "Zen" place

Affirmative

Teach the child to tell themselves positive statements:

I can handle this.

I am better than this.

This is not worth losing privileges over.

Move Away

Teach the child to say something like:

"Thanks for sharing your opinion and move away."

Teach the child to not make eye contact when saying the above statement.

Ice it down....

Know how you can add ice to a hot cup of cocoa, and it cools it down to "just right"? Or ice an inflamed muscle and it calms down.

Learn what to say to bring the child down to "just right."

For example:

If the child likes to set up the overhead projector and you see they are about to go over the edge, ask them to set up the overhead projector for you.

Music calms the inner "beast"

We all have times when our inner beast comes out.

Share with the student what you do....

Notes:

Response Feedback

Cool Down Techniques

Instead of saying "Sit Down" Use;

Choices. The University of Michigan says offering two equal choices gives a 98% compliance rate. Pair that with the research on right ear preference and the student is most likely to comply. (http://hi.baidu.com/esler/blog/item/4727521cc29c8a8286d6b6ff.html)

Compassion. Handle all problems with compassion. Instead of saying, "Why did you rip up that paper?" Say, "I can totally understand why you felt like ripping up that paper." This will bring down the brick wall that is ready to raise and then you can say, "But, we can't allow students to behave in such a manner and here is how you will make restitution for that action."

Low Self-Esteem

When students are in kindergarten 80% of them have high self-esteem. When students are in fifth grade 20% of them have high self-esteem. When students are in high school five percent of them have high self-esteem (Canfield, 2009).

The Four P's for Raising Self Esteem

- Public Relations
- Proficiency
- Power
- Philanthropy

There is a worksheet at the back of this book. We have implemented the Four P's of Raising Self-Esteem with over 1000 students in Kansas and Oklahoma and have yet to find a student who did not respond. Our baseline was based on two factors: student grades and target behavior. We wanted grades to go up and target behaviors to go down. We implemented the Four P's for one month and measured grades and target behaviors again. In each case, there was a positive change in one or both of these factors. The key is consistency of implementing all four quadrants of the Four P's. (Worksheet on page 83)

Here is a PowerPoint on the Four P's- Go to www.behaviordoctor.org. Click on materials and go to PowerPoint- scroll to the Four P's Presentation

TIPP behavior in your favor:

Teach it

Imprint it by modeling it

Practice it

Praise it when you see it

How to **CARE** for behavior

Control

How can I make it appear the child has more control over situations?

Attention

Does the child want the adult attention or peer attention?

Revenge

What social skills can we give the child to help them refrain from reactive strategies?

Escape

Why does the child want to get out of work or get away from a situation? (low self-esteem, inadequate skills, etc.)

Functional Behavior Assessment- FBA

Conduct data using the FBA Data Tool and then make a plan to address the function behind the behavior using the triggers and impacTs that are feeding this behavior. It is impossible to have a one size fits all plan for all students with ODD. Every student is unique.

The multi-modal plan. Does not just put one statement in place:

Consider if your doctor said, "Get better." No different to tell a child with a medical diagnosis to "Be Good." (it only works for ET)

Label appropriate behavior. Instead of telling the child what "NOT" to do- tell them what to do by labelling it when you see it.

I like the way you…. (the more you say- the more you'll see.)

Get rid of the totalitarian rules:

Don't _____

No _____

Quit _____

Stop _____

answer to a question. Please teach me a trick to make it easy.

Cool down technique for YOU. Children with ODD seem to be able to send us from frontal cortex to brain stem in 20 seconds flat. This happens because we have been trained to think, "I must react immediately to this situation because that's what we do." The truth is…we don't think best when we are upset. Train yourself to do the following: Use the late-night host technique. If you don't have enough information yet ask an open-ended question like:

"Tell me more."

When you do deal with it:

Handle all problems with compassion first.

> "Oh, man I can totally understand why you felt like doing that.
>
> But the rules for that are x, y, and z at this school.
>
> So, we'll see you in detention on what day?
>
> After that, let's get together and talk.
>
> Be sure to come see me the next day."

Use a Point System. How many of you collect frequent flyer miles or reward points for hotels?

It makes you want to engage in a particular behavior. See the Student Teacher Rating Sheet on pages 71-79.

Check In- Check Out Program. The most critical factor influencing the development of pro-social behavior is the attachment to at least one pro-social adult who believes in the child and provides unconditional acceptance and support (Horner et.al., 2008; Hawkins, 1995; Bernard, 1995; Brooks, 1994; & Katz, 1995).

Kids with ODD- First instinct is to not trust adults

TUMS for the ODD Child:

Touch them- High five or gentle touch on forearm when talking to them. Message: We touch people we like.

Use their name

Make eye contact

Smile

Notes:

In order to see any behavior, change, we need to address the Triple T's.

Trigger	**Target**	**impacT**
What set the behavior in motion? Could be a direct antecedent (something that happened right before) or could be a setting event (something that happened in the near distant past)	What is the behavior you would like to target for change?	What is the student gaining or escaping by engaging in this behavior?
Environmental Change/Cue	**Replacement Behavior**	**Response Feedback**
What can you do to set this student up for success? What cues can you set up in the environment to help the student remember the necessary behavior changes?	What replacement behaviors have you taught the student? This can be done through: • Modeling • Peer mentoring • Video modeling • Social Stories • Video self-modeling • Counseling	How can you change your own reaction, so you feed the replacement behavior with the desired impacT and extinguish the Target behavior by withholding the desired impacT?

Environmental Change: 🌐

Replacement Behavior: ★

Response Feedback: 🔓

Autism Spectrum Disorders

The numbers are growing:

1950's 1- in 10,000

2013 1 in 50 (CDC- parent report)

2016- Most used statistic by professionals 1 in 68

Movie about Carly Fleischmann can be downloaded here:

http://www.youtube.com/watch?v=xMBzJleeOno

Just because I don't talk-Does not mean I don't have something to say!!!

(Photo by Elizabeth Davenport)

Autism

Autism is considered a spectrum disorder. Which basically means, if you've met one student with autism, you've met one student with autism. The strengths of each student with autism are as varied as they are in any other category.

Autism can present as a student who is non-verbal. This does not mean the student is not intelligent. As educators, we should always make the presumption that the student understands every single thing we are saying and inflecting with our tone and body language. Give the benefit of the doubt. You may see students flap, rub their fingers together, rock, make humming noises, and make noise with something else. As we learned in Carly's video, this is to create output to cover up input that overwhelms them.

Autism can also present as a student who has a strong vocal knowledge of a particular topic of interest. This can be used to your advantage by using those interests to engage the student in the subjects you are teaching. To learn more about autism, here are some books that you might find interesting:

Asperger/Autism:

the curious incident of the dog in the night-time by mark haddon

Look Me in the Eye by John Elder Robison

Be Different: Adventures of a Free-Range Aspergian with Practical Advice for Aspergians, Misfits, Families & Teachers by John Elder Robison

Born on a Blue Day: Inside the Mind of an Autistic Savant by Daniel Tammet

The Exceptional Life of Jay Turnbull: Disability and Dignity in America 1967-2009 By Rud Turnbull

Brains, Trains, and Video Games: Living the Autism Life by Alicia Hart, Brianne Bolin, Ewan Nees and Tera Swang

Environmental Changes

Overstimulation. Think about all five senses. Imagine hearing the humming of the fluorescent light, the motor of the overhead projector, the bees buzzing outside, someone scratching their skin, chair legs scooting on the floor, and someone tapping their pencil all at the same volume and ten times louder than a neuro-typical hears them. Many children with autism are hyper-acoustic. They hear everything extremely loud and cannot cypher out what is important and what is not. For an excellent take on what this feels like watch:

http://www.youtube.com/watch?v=KmDGvquzn2k You only have to watch 2 minutes of this- imagine what it is like 24 hours a day.

Noises. Minimize- carpet on the floor helps

- Tennis balls on bottom of chair and table legs
- Seat the student away from the overhead projector for the Smartboard
- Seat the student away from the door and hallway noise
- Seat the student away from fluorescent lights above
- Keep noise to a minimum

Many students who are bothered by noise levels have a very difficult time in the gymnasium and lunchroom. Think of providing ear protection that doesn't single the student out. For instance, the ability to listen to an old iPod with soft music or background white noise will help them override the urge to run from loud noisy areas. Some students have hyperacusis. This means they hear approximately ten times louder than most. For more information on Decreased Sound Tolerance and Hyperacusis try this website: http://www.hyperacusis.net/

Hallway noise can be difficult for students as well. The pool noodle idea under smells also decreases noise coming from the hallway if the door is shut. Discount stores have larger pool noodles in the summer time and these are ideal.

Lighting. The flickering of the fluorescent lights can be a distraction. Consider writing a grant to put in www.huelight.net panels. The panels are about $20 apiece and all but stop the flicker from coming through.

- Use lamps around the room with incandescent light bulbs and leave overhead lights off
- Use natural light as much as possible

Besides the flicker of the 100 hertz bulbs, which flicker 100 times per second, they emit a high-pitched hum that some students can hear. As much as possible, dim the lights in the classroom. At least dim them over the desk of the students who are sensitive to light and sound.

Smells. If your classroom is near the cafeteria or the pool in the gym area, consider using a draft dodger. You can make your own for a dollar. Get a pool noodle at the dollar store and cut it in half. Slip it into an old pillow case which has been made narrower by sewing down the middle and cutting off the extra half. Slide one pool noodle on each side of the door. This will decrease the smells coming into your room.

- Consider not wearing perfume. Even body lotion can bother students with sensory integration issues. Students with Traumatic Brain Injury (TBI) can be highly sensitive to smell and it can trigger a migraine headache.

- Do not use plug in room deodorizers or spray room deodorizer
- To eliminate dank musty smells, sprinkle baking soda on the carpet and then vacuum it up

Textures. If a child is acting uncomfortable, check out what they are wearing:
- Seams on socks
- Tags in the back of clothing
- Itchy material
- Seams in clothing
- Think about what they are sitting on
- Allow them to bring house slippers from home and take off their shoes and socks in the room
- Talk to parents about comfortable clothing choices

Transitions. Anything that is a change is a transition. Changing classes, changing activities, changing people can be a huge event for a child with autism if they are not prepared for the change. We used a **PowerPoint** relationship narrative to help students and housemates with changes that were coming each day. For samples Go to www.behaviordoctor.org. Click on materials then scroll to Relationship Narratives.

These can be developed with pictures of the student and recordings of the student. They can be narrated and saved a PowerPoint shows .pps and then transferred onto a Palm Pilot or iPad or iPhone for a student using a simple program called DataViz. You can download a free version of DataViz here: https://www.dataviz.com/DTG_iphone.html

- Remember to make one for students when they transition from one school to the next.

Some great websites you might like:

www.wrongplanet.net

http://zacbrowser.com

http://www.amctheatres.com/programs/sensory-friendly-films

http://sensorystar.com

http://sensorysmarts.com/helpful_websites.html

Food for thought

People with disabilities do not lose their jobs (post-secondary education) because of failure to perform required tasks, but because of fitting in socially within the workplace (Brickey, Campbell & Browning, 1985; Butterworth & Stauch, 1994; Chadsey, 2007; Greenspan & Shoulz, 1981)

Employers have these expectations for their employees:

- Interacting with co-workers at breaks
- Requesting assistance
- Providing assistance

- Responding appropriately to constructive criticism
- Appropriate tone of voice
- Appropriate level of voice
- Appropriate voicing of concerns
- Appropriate adherence to others' personal space
- Socially appropriate interrupting techniques

(Social Validation Studies- DADD June 2012)

Notes:

Replacement Behavior

Video Self-Modeling ★

The Siskin Institute has a wonderful video on https://www.youtube.com/watch?v=nZv9sBtQbHE this is a sample of how to set up a video for a student. The examples are:

- Tommy: A young man who was monosyllabic. They took a lot of video and then spliced it together to make it look like he was saying complete sentences.
- Lilian: A little girl who reacted to students instead of playing with them. They took a lot of video and spliced it together to make it appear she was participating in reciprocal play.
- Emily: A young girl who only ate four foods. They took several days of video and made it appear that she was eating something from each area on her tray.

We take video of students on and off the spectrum to create video self-modeling solutions. We ask the parents to show the video at home in the morning before the child comes to school. We show the video to the student during the day as needed for booster shots. We ask the parents to show the video again at night and ask their child how their day went remembering to use all the labeled behaviors. This has been very effective and is research based.

LaSpata, M., Carter, C.W., Johnson, W.L., & McGill, R.J., (2016) Evaluation Video Self-Modeling Treatment Outcomes: Differentiating between Statistically and Clinically Significant Change. *Contemporary School Psychology.* v20, n2, p170-182

Losinski, M., Wiseman, N., White, S.A., & Balluch, F. (2016) A Meta-Analysis of Video-Modeling Based Interventions for Reduction of Challenging Behaviors for Students with EBD. *Journal of Special Education.* V49, N4, P243-252

Gelbar, N. W., Anderson, C., McCarthy, S., & Buggey, T. (2012) Video Self-Modeling as an Intervention Strategy for Individuals with Autism Spectrum Disorders. *Psychology in the Schools.* V 49, N1, p15-22

Incredible Five Point Scale ★

By Kari Dunn Buron and Mitzi Curtis

From their website to order- here is the description:

https://www.aapcpublishing.net/aapc-bookstore/product-viewer.aspx?slug=The-Incredible-5-Point-Scale
The Incredible 5-Point Scale:
The Significantly Improved and Expanded Second Edition. Supporting emotional regulation has become a critical priority in effective programming for students with ASD. The Incredible 5-Point Scale was one of the first practical supports to help all partners recognize and teach students to become aware of their state of regulation. The Significantly Improved and Expanded Second Edition of the now classic resource expands on the core idea of the original scale by providing current clinical examples of how to use the scale across different age groups and functioning levels. New scales are offered specifically designed for young children and those individuals with more classic presentations of autism, including an expanded use of the Anxiety

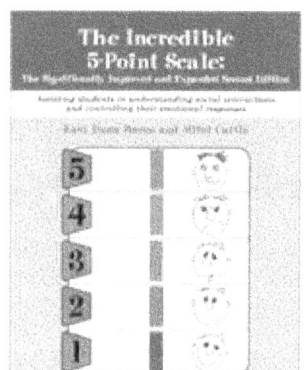 Curve. Another addition is a list of goals and objectives related to incorporating scales in students' IEP's.

We ordered this book for the Behavioral Intervention Program and we used it all the time with students in our care. We highly recommend it.

PowerPoint Relationship Narratives

To teach social skills, an inexpensive tool to use would be PowerPoint lessons on how to interact with other students. For samples of these, go to www.behaviordoctor.org under materials and scroll to Relationship Narratives.

The relationship narratives on Behavior Doctor are generic. Be sure to put in real pictures of your students and use their voice or one that would be equivalent in the PowerPoint. Save it as a PowerPoint Show and it will run like a movie. This is age appropriate for all Pre-K through Adult.

PowerPoint Relationship Narratives

- To communicate change in schedule
- To teach schedule and routines
- To use as a visual schedule
- To teach appropriate behaviors
- To entertain for rewards
- To teach reading

Aggressive Behaviors

Behavior is communication; however, we cannot let children with autism bite, scratch, kick, or hit themselves or others. Here are some redirections that have worked for other children:

Biting

Give the child a chewy tube or a chew tube on a keychain and direct them to bite this when they feel like biting. If they bite themselves put it where they will see it- keep it clipped to their belt loop. If they bite you or another adult keep it clipped to the adult target and direct them to bite that when they feel the need to bite. Reward them with praise and or a tangible when they bite the tube instead of themselves or others. This usually stems from a sensory need and when they get overloaded, they go for the first thing.

Plopping

When a child drops to the floor and refuses to move, we call that plopping. There could be two different functions to this but if it happens frequently and at no apparent time interval then it is probably for attention. Put a mat up near the child so that no one can make eye contact with the child and sit them out. Make sure it is not set up in a way that would make the child feel claustrophobic. Act like it is no big deal to you that they are on the floor. This won't work if the function is escape. If they are trying to escape a particular activity try to sandwich the non-preferred activity between one that follows that is extremely rewarding. Use and First-Then schedule to show them what is coming next.

Pinching

Place a clothespin on the spot where the child usually pinches you. During times of non-stress direct them to pinch the clothespin. Reward them with praise or tangibles for pinching the clothespin. When they do forget and pinch you remind them to pinch the clothespin. Once they have mastered pinching the clothespin on you, move the clothespin to their own clothing and direct them to pinch that when they feel the need to pinch. Many times, this started as a sensory behavior and the payoff from the adult or child who got pinched reinforced the behavior. If it is not for sensory, use a token economy for using their skills to get attention in appropriate ways.

Tantrums

Children who have tantrums frequently, tend to build up momentum until they don't realize where they are in time or space. It's very hard to come back to reality once you have left the gravitational pull. We have used bean bag chairs to act as shock absorbers for the tantrum energy. The child is directed to sit in the beanbag and communicate a want or need. They are rewarded for this activity during a non-stress time. Once they are beginning the stages of tantrum they are taken to the beanbag and returned there every time they get up until they learn to stay in the beanbag during times of stress. Please note they are never manhandled or picked up to be taken to the beanbag. This will infuriate the child.

We start with picture exchange communication cards (PECS) and eventually, they are given a communication device to let them communicate what it is that is bothering them. A blanket is near so the child can put the blanket over their head if they are on sensory overload and need to escape lights and sounds.

Eloping

Eloping is a behavior that we get requests for help on frequently. We have to shape this behavior by reinforcing the appropriate behavior. The best video for demonstrating this is:

https://www.youtube.com/watch?v=qKZaKK3pTkQ It is called "Elopement Robbie". I like this video because they show the wrong and the right way to shape a behavior.

Notes:

Response Feedback

How we respond to a child with autism when they have their first behavior determines whether we see it again or not. Many people do not realize how quickly a behavior can become "set". Here is a generic example. The first time Jay came to the house on Alabama Street, he was shown around the main floor and then taken upstairs up the carpeted steps. He was shown around upstairs and then taken down the front wooden steps on the other side of the home. From that point forward, he would only go up the carpeted steps and only go down the wooden steps.

We worked with a non-verbal child once who had temper tantrums every time, he got off the bus to see his mother who was waiting on the front porch. It took us quite some time to figure this out, but the first two times he got off the bus, his mother was so glad to see him that she got down on her knees at his level and hugged him. After the first few times, she just stood on the porch and waited for him to walk up to her. Once she started going out to greet him and got down on his level, he was fine and had no more tantrums. We have to really think about how we are responding to everything and make sure we are not setting patterns we do not want to repeat.

Label Appropriate Behavior

We brought students into the clinic and the only intervention we used was labeling appropriate behavior. "I like the way you are sitting in your chair." "Good sitting in your chair." Instead of saying "Don't, Stop, Quit, and No", it is important for us to label the appropriate behavior when we see it and tell them what to do instead of telling them what not to do.

Token Economy

Token economy systems work well with most students. We have to figure out what floats their boat. For students with non-verbal skills, we can do a Stimulus Choice Assessment. We worked with a middle school student once who previously had done nothing as far as productive work. We found out he liked pretty girls. The cheerleaders practiced the last hour of the day. He earned tokens for working during the day. He worked 15 minutes and then earned a five-minute break. If he came back from his break with only one prompt, he earned a token. At the end of the day, if he had enough tokens, he could go watch the cheerleader's practice. It was worth giving up a little time at the end of the day to get all the work out of him that we accomplished by using this token economy system.

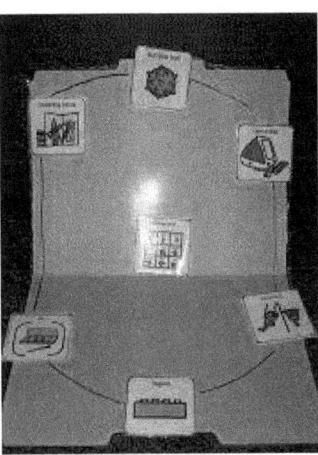

This is a choice folder. The student puts the picture of what they want to work for in the center of the folder. After 15 minutes of work, they earn the choice chosen for a five-minute break.

Notes:

To Listen to The Entire Dolls in Your Classroom Series:

www.blogtalkradio.com/behaviordoctor

- Ants in the Pants Arthur
- Bite Me Barbie
- Cussing Cookie Monster
- Debating Dora
- Eloping Elmo
- Fighting Fred Flintstone
- Gregarious Gingerbread Man
- Hypochondriac Holly Hobby
- Investigating Inspector Gadget
- Jumping G.I. Joe
- Karate Ken
- Lazy Leonardo
- Messy Mr. Magoo
- Non-compliant Nemo
- Ostrich Ollie
- Polly Pickpockets
- Quibbling Quick Draw McGraw
- Rude Raggedy Ann
- Space Cadet Skipper
- Tantrum Trolls
- Undermining Underdog
- Violent Velma
- Wandering Waldo
- Xanax Xena
- You Can't Make Me: Yogi
- Zeroed out Zorro

Workbook Pages:

1	2	3	4	5	6	7	8	9	10
11	12	13	14	15	16	17	18	19	20
21	22	23	24	25	26	27	28	29	30
31	32	33	34	35	36	37	38	39	40
41	42	43	44	45	46	47	48	49	50
51	52	53	54	55	56	57	58	59	60
61	62	63	64	65	66	67	68	69	70
71	72	73	74	75	76	77	78	79	80
81	82	83	84	85	86	87	88	89	90
91	92	93	94	95	96	97	98	99	100

Sample- Multiples of Four- Students start to see the pattern in a base 10 number system:

1	2	3	4	5	6	7	8	9	10
11	12	13	14	15	16	17	18	19	20
21	22	23	24	25	26	27	28	29	30
31	32	33	34	35	36	37	38	39	40
41	42	43	44	45	46	47	48	49	50
51	52	53	54	55	56	57	58	59	60
61	62	63	64	65	66	67	68	69	70
71	72	73	74	75	76	77	78	79	80
81	82	83	84	85	86	87	88	89	90
91	92	93	94	95	96	97	98	99	100

Student Teacher Rating Sheet

Student Name: _____

Date: _____

	Hour One		Hour Two		Hour Three		Hour Four		Hour Five		Hour Six		Hour Seven	
	T	S	T	S	T	S	T	S	T	S	T	S	T	S
Keep hands and feet to self														
Respect personal space between each other														
Turn work in on time														
Accepts Score (Teacher only)														
Total														

Total Points Earned Today: _____ out of 84 possible

Prize Earned: _____

Parent Signature: _____

Prize tomorrow for 67-84= _____

Prize tomorrow for 58-66=_____

Prize tomorrow for 50-57=_____

Prize for 49 or lower=_____

Behavior Doctor Seminars®™ 2019

Student Copy of Teacher Student Rating Sheet- This sheet should be laminated so the student can reuse.

	Hour One	Hour Two	Hour Three	Hour Four	Hour Five	Hour Six	Hour Seven
Keep hands and feet to self	My score	My score	My score	My score	My score	My score	My score
Respect personal space between each other	My score	My score	My score	My score	My score	My score	My score
Turn work in on time	My score	My score	My score	My score	My score	My score	My score
Total from teacher's paper after we match							

3 = I give myself a 3 if the teacher did not have to remind me about the rule for each behavior I am working on.

2 = I give myself a 2 if the teacher had to remind me a few times about the rule for each behavior I am working on.

1 = I give myself a 1 if I did not remember to follow the rule at all and the teacher had to remind me more than a couple of times.

Be Honest: Remember you earn points based on matching the teacher's score!

Young Child copy of Teacher Student Rating Sheet- This sheet should be laminated so the student can reuse.

	Hour One	Hour Two	Hour Three	Hour Four	Hour Five	Hour Six	Hour Seven
Keep hands and feet to self	My score ☺ 😐 ☹	My score ☺ 😐 ☹	My score ☺ 😐 ☹	My score ☺ 😐 ☹	My score ☺ 😐 ☹	My score ☺ 😐 ☹	My score ☺ 😐 ☹
Respect personal space between each other	My score ☺ 😐 ☹	My score ☺ 😐 ☹	My score ☺ 😐 ☹	My score ☺ 😐 ☹	My score ☺ 😐 ☹	My score ☺ 😐 ☹	My score ☺ 😐 ☹
Turn work in on time	My score ☺ 😐 ☹	My score ☺ 😐 ☹	My score ☺ 😐 ☹	My score ☺ 😐 ☹	My score ☺ 😐 ☹	My score ☺ 😐 ☹	My score ☺ 😐 ☹
Teacher writes points on sheet for them							

Behavior Doctor Seminars®™ 2019

Free or Inexpensive Rewards for Parents

Young Children

1. Assist the parent with a household chore
2. Send an email to a relative telling them what a good job they had done on a project at school. In other words, email Aunt Linda and tell her about the "A" you got on your spelling test.
3. Get to decorate paper placemats for the dining room table for dinner that evening
4. Get to choose what is fixed for dinner that night- example: "You get to choose; I can make tacos or meatloaf. Which do you want me to fix?"
5. Get to help parent fix dinner- shell peas, peel potatoes, make art out of vegetables, make ants on a log etc.
6. Get to be the first person to share 3 stars and a wish at the dinner table (3 good things that happened that day and one thing they wish had gone better.)
7. Get to create a family night activity- roller skating, hiking in the park, picnic dinner on the living room floor or under the dining room table with blankets over the top.
8. Camp out in the backyard with a parent.
9. Get a car ride to or from school instead of the bus
10. Get to have a picture framed for mom or dad's office
11. Get to choose the game the family plays together that night
12. Get to choose the story the family reads out loud together (read the classics)
13. Get to go with a parent to volunteer at a retirement home (the children will get tons of attention)
14. Get to gather old toys and take to a shelter for children who have nothing
15. Get to ask friends to bring dog and cat food to their birthday party instead of toys that will break. Take the food to a shelter the day after as a reward. They will get a ton of attention from the staff.
16. Bury treasures in a sandbox for the child to find. Put letters in plastic Easter eggs and they have to put the letters together that spell treat the child will receive. (Ideas: a walk with grandma, bike riding at the park, etc.)
17. Make special mud pies in the backyard with mom or dad or have a family contest to see who can make the best mud pie.
18. Dig shapes in the sandbox and then decorate with items found around the house. Pour inexpensive plaster of Paris into the shape and wait to dry. When it's pulled out it will be a sandy relief that can be hung on the wall (if you remember to put a paper clip in the plaster of Paris on the top before it dries ☺)
19. Get to go shopping with a parent as an only child. Give them a special task to look for something that you are seeking. For example: "Here's a picture of a blue blouse that I'm trying to find. Help me look for something that looks like this."
20. Take all the kids to grandma and grandpa's except one and let that child stay home with mom and dad and be "only child" for the weekend. The other kids will get spoiled with lots of attention by grandma and grandpa and the "only child" will get lots of attention from mom and dad. (If you don't have grandma and grandpa nearby- trade with another family taking turns to keep each other's children.)
21. Download a fun recipe and let your child help you make that recipe as a surprise for the rest of the family that evening. (Put up signs that say, "Secret Cooking in Progress". Must have special pass to enter the kitchen.

22. Surprise your child with a scavenger hunt around the house. If they read, give them written clues hinting as to where the next card is hiding. At the end have them find a note that tells them their big prize. (If your child can't read, you can use pictures.)
23. Make a story on the computer with your child using Microsoft's PowerPoint program. Let your child be the star of the story.
24. Let your child take the digital camera out in the back yard and then come back in and turn those pictures into a story on the computer. Help them print off their book for a distant family member.
25. Go outside and collect cool leaves and flowers. Come inside and put those leaves and flowers between two sheets of wax paper. The parent will iron these two sheets together and create placemats for everyone in the family for the evening.
26. Start a family story at the dinner table and each person in the family has to tell a part of the story. The child being rewarded gets to start and end the story.
27. Let your child earn 5 minutes of either staying up later or sleeping in in the morning. Use that time to read together if they stay up later.
28. Play secretary and let your child dictate a story to you. Type up the story and send it out to some relatives who will call them and tell them how much they liked the story.
29. Write a story for your child where the child or their personal hero is a character in the story.
30. Change the screen saver on your computer to say, "My child is the greatest." ...or something that would make them feel good about themselves. Do this at your office and then take a picture of it or take your child to your office on the weekend and let them see it.
31. Let your child help you do the laundry and then pay them with a special dessert for dinner. Be sure to say, "Since you helped me save time by helping me fold the laundry, I have time to make this special dessert for dinner."
32. Help your child organize their room giving them a mnemonic to help them remember where things go- for instance teach them the color order of the rainbow and then teach them to hang up their clothes in color groups matching the order of the rainbow (ROYGBIV). Later on, when you catch them hanging up their clothes in the correct place draw a "rainbow" award for their good work and put it on their door as a surprise when they come home.
33. Have the bedroom fairy come while they are at school and choose the bedroom that is the neatest. Hang a fairy from the doorway of the room that is the neatest and that person gets to sit in "Dad's chair" to read that night. (Or something that would be appropriate at your house).
34. Mystery grab bag. Take an old pillow case and put slips of paper inside listing some of the prizes on this page and let the child draw out the prize they are going to get for their behavior reward.
35. Let your child dictate where you drive on the way home from a location. In other words, they have to tell you turn left here...turn right here. If they happen to steer you into a Baskin Robbins Ice Cream Parlor, it wouldn't be a horrible thing to stop and have a family treat together.
36. Give your child a special piece of jewelry that belongs to you to keep and wear for the day. (Nothing that costs a lot of money- but something that looks like it is special to you.) The child will feel special all day long.
37. Take your children to the library one at a time and give them special one on one time at the library checking out books or listening to stories.
38. Sign your child up for acting lessons (they have to have earned this privilege). Many universities offer free acting classes on the weekend for children.

39. Take your child to an art gallery and then have them draw a picture of their favorite painting or statue. Possibly stage a mini art gallery tour of the child's work for relatives who are coming to visit. Serve cheese and grape juice.
40. Take your child to the university astronomy lab. (It is usually free). Help them place stars on the ceiling of their room in their favorite constellation. If possible, they could paint the stars with "glow in the dark" paint.
41. Take your child on a nature walk and collect rocks. Bring the rocks back home and have a contest painting the rocks to look like animals.
42. Have your child collect some toys they have outgrown. Clean up the toys and take them to a local hospital children's ward and donate the toys to the ward. The child will get lots of attention and feel good.
43. Go to your local appliance store and ask them to save a refrigerator box for you. The next time your child earns a reward, give them the box and help them plan and decorate the box to turn it into anything their imagination desires.
44. Make **Papier-mâché** Halloween masks by taking punch ball balloons and spreading the paper strips over the balloon shape. Make noses, horns, tongues whatever they desire and then paint when dry. You will have a unique and free Halloween costume and you will have given your child tons of attention.
45. Find an old-fashioned popcorn popper (not an air popper). Spread an old sheet out on the living room floor, put a little oil in the popper and then have your children sit outside the perimeter of the sheet. Put a few kernels of popcorn in the popper and watch them fly up in the air. The kids will love watching this. For a special treat pour cinnamon sugar on the popcorn after it pops.
46. Find some light balsa wood and create a boat powered by a rubber band and paper clip paddle wheel. Make a unique sail and take the boat to a creek or lake nearby and help your child launch their boat. Be sure to take a butterfly net to retrieve the boat when it goes downstream. (Proactively, you could put an eye hook on the front of the boat and attach some fishing line to it so it can be brought back to shore.
47. Take your child fishing. It's a great place to have some really in-depth conversations.
48. Take your child for a ride looking for items that start with each letter of the alphabet. Take the child's picture in front of each item that starts with that letter and then put it together as an ABC Book. For example: "This is Johnny in front of Applebees." "This is Johnny in front of BlockBuster." And so on....
49. Check with your local humane society and see if they allow children under 18 to volunteer to feed and water the animals. (Some shelters only allow adults over 18). Let your child earn the privilege of going to the shelter to feed and water the animals. Perhaps they can walk a small dog or pet a cat.
50. Take your child to the local fire department. As long as they are not busy, they will be glad to show the child around and give them some great attention. Most children have seen a fire truck, but few have actually gone to the fire department to see what it looks like.
51. Play the "Gatekeeper Game" with your child
52. Tell your children you have a surprise performance for them. Get a stocking cap and lay on a sturdy table with your head hanging chin up in the air. Cover all of your face with the stocking cap except your chin and mouth. Draw two eyeballs on your chin and then lip sync to a silly song. It looks really funny, like a little headed person with a big mouth singing. Then let your child put on a performance for you.
53. Play hide and go seek in your house in the dark. Turn out all the lights and have everyone hide. One person is "it" and they have to go around the house and find the people who are hiding. It's really a great way to help your children not be afraid of the dark. You can limit it to one or two rooms if your children are young.

54. Ask your children if they'd rather have a dollar a day for thirty days or a penny a day that doubles each day for 30 days. In other words, on day one 1 cent, day two 2 more cents, day three 4 cents and so on. Once they decide then help them figure out which one would have been the better deal. $10,737,418.23 at the end of 30 days with the double the pennies per day.
55. Give your child a nice piece of Manila paper and some wax crayons. Have them color a design on every inch of the paper- could be stripes or wavy lines- whatever they desire. Then have them cover the entire page with black crayon. They color over the entire page. Then give them a paper clip and have them open one end and scratch a cool design into the black crayon. The colors underneath will show through. Do an art gallery tour and have tea and cookies after looking at the different pictures.
56. Teach your child how to throw a football, shoot a basket, kick a field goal, hit a baseball, and putt a golf ball. Then for fun, switch hands and try to do all of those things with the opposite side of the body.
57. Find an old croquet set- probably on Ebay. Set up croquet in your yard and challenge your child to a game of croquet. The winning child gets to choose what the family eats for dinner.
58. Turn your dining room table into a cave by covering it with blankets, quilts and sheets that cover the top and sides down to the floor. Lay inside the cave and draw picture by flashlight to hang on the wall of the cave- just like the caveman drawings. You can safety pin the pictures to the "cave walls".
59. Have a talent night for the family. Have everyone keep it a secret what they are doing and then perform for each other.
60. Teach your child how to darn a sock and then turn it into a magical sock puppet. Put on puppet shows for each other.
61. Take a tension curtain rod and put it in the door frame with some old curtains attached. Let your child put on a talent show for you as they enter through the curtain.
62. Attach cork panels to a wall in the kitchen or put in a large picture frame and put a special piece of art, poetry, or an exceptional paper on the board and have the entire family view and comment at dinner on the highlighted piece.
63. Let your child design thank you cards, birthday cards, or holiday cards and use them to send to friends and relatives. Make sure they sign their work.
64. Buy your child an inexpensive digital camera and have them take pictures and then gather the family with popcorn and watch the video on your television by hooking the camera to the television or upload to the computer and attach the computer to the television. Have everyone choose a favorite photo and talk about it.
65. Have a date night with your child as an only child. Take your child out to dinner and a play or a movie.

Teenagers

1. A gallon of paint is inexpensive. Let the child choose the color and help them paint their room. You can also buy mistake paint (colors that didn't work out for others) and let the child paint a mural on their bedroom wall.
2. Teenagers need extra-curricular activities; however, these activities are expensive. Work out a deal with the karate teacher, horse stable, art teacher, sport coach etc. Offer to

Behavior Doctor Seminars®™ 2019

provide transportation, house cleaning duties once a month, or precooked meals to get a discount on these classes for your teenager.
3. Teenagers have a difficult time with their emotions. Download yoga lessons from online and do yoga breathing exercises together as a family. Talk to your child about using these techniques when they feel tense at school.
4. Make a deal. If your child maintains the grades you agree upon, does not have any unnecessary absences, and has been agreeable, allow them to take a mental health day and stay home on a day you are home as well. Go window shopping together, fishing, go-kart riding, or whatever would float your child's boat. My mother did this with us when we were children and I still remember these days fondly.
5. Let your teenager play their music during dinner and talk to you about why they like each song that plays.
6. Watch an old black and white classic movie together and talk about how movies have changed. My children loved "Harvey" with Jimmy Stewart when they were teenagers.
7. Write half a story or poem and let your teenager write the other half. Submit the story for publication.
8. Scan your teenager's papers or art work and have them bound in a book (www.lulu.com has inexpensive binding available). Present the book to your teenager at a special dinner.
9. Make a scrap book of your teenager and their friends with ticket stubs and pictures and present at a surprise party.
10. Save your change for a year. Let your teenager choose what to do with that money. One family that I know saved enough to take a family of six to Disneyland.
11. One of the greatest gifts you can give to a teenager is to teach them charity. Sign up to work in a soup kitchen, nursing home, or other similar area and work with them once a month.
12. Organize a neighborhood football or basketball game "oldies" vs "youngsters" or "men" vs. "women" and then have a block barbecue afterwards.
13. Let them drive the "good" car for a special occasion.
14. Surprise them with their favorite dessert for no special reason.
15. Write a story about the 20 things you love about them. Include fun pictures.
16. Choose a family member of the month and make a poster of them. Let them choose Friday night dinners for the month.
17. Teach your children how to play a game like *Spoons, Canasta, Poker*, etc. and have a family game night.
18. Turn out all the lights in the house and play hide and go seek in the dark. The person that can stay hidden the longest gets to choose the movie the family watches on Saturday night.
19. Hire your child to be an interior decorator and using only items available in the house, redo a room in the house.
20. Do your own *Trading Spaces*. Parents redecorate the teen's bedroom and the teen redecorates the parent's bedroom.
21. Use plastic Easter eggs and put dollar amounts in the eggs on slips of paper and number the eggs with a permanent marker. Play *Deal or No Deal* with one of the parents playing the banker.
22. Help your teenager study for a test by downloading a free *Who Wants to be a Millionaire* PowerPoint game and put the answers to your teenagers' test into the game and then play to help them study.
23. Tape record your student's study questions onto a tape recorder for them so they can listen to them while they are going to sleep.
24. Make flash cards for your student's exams to help them study for a big exam.

Behavior Doctor Seminars®™ 2019

25. Help your teenager organize their notebook using color coded folders for each subject and pocket folders for study cards.
26. Hide positive messages all over your teenager's room, in their books they use at home (you don't want them to get embarrassed at school), on their bathroom mirror, etc.
27. Watch Jeopardy and give each family member a pad of post it notes or index cards. Have everyone write down what they think the answer is and keep points. The person who wins gets to pick what the family does as an activity that weekend.
28. Do some research for your teenager. For example, if your teen is studying Greek Mythology go to the library and check out all the books on Greek Mythology for them or download some appropriate materials from the Internet (be careful of the Internet as some information is not correct).
29. Take your teen to a museum, on a nature walk, to a sporting event, whatever would float their boat. It's the time you spend with them that is important and there are many free events you can attend.
30. Make a special mix CD for your teen of their favorite songs. You can upload i-tunes and then copy their own CD's into the program and mix and match their favorite songs onto one CD, so they don't have to flip through CD's to listen to their favorite songs.
31. Have a contest to see who can find something that no one in the family can guess what it is. For example, a shirt stays, or the inside spring to a toy, things that might not be recognizable away from their use.
32. Have everyone come to the table with a quote and then a contest to see who can guess who made the quote famous.
33. Surprise your teen with a scavenger hunt all over the house when they get home from school. Make the clues hard to figure out. I always had a little prize at the end like baseball cards.
34. Let your teen host the training of a guide dog. This will teach them responsibility and give them a sense of pride.
35. Help your teen become a big brother or sister to a child who needs a mentor. There is no greater gift you can give yourself than that of service to someone in need.

For 32 pages of Free Rewards for Educators follow this link:

Go to www.behaviordoctor.org – click on materials download- then scroll to "reinforcements"

Social Autopsy (Based on the ideas from Rick LaVoie, 2005)

Here's what was going on:	Here's what I did that caused a social error:	Here's what happened when I did that:	Here's what I should do to make things right:	Here's my plan for next time it happens:

Behavior Doctor Seminars®™ 2019

Three Stars and a Wish (Journal Entry)

 One thing that went really well this week:

 Second thing that went really well this week:

 Third thing that went really well this week:

 One thing I wish had gone differently this week:

Subject _____ - Name _____

My Grades

		Assignment	Assignment	Assignment	Assignment	Assignment
A	90-100%					
B	80-89%					
C	70-79%					
D	60-69%					
F	50-59%					
	40-49%					
	30-39%					
	20-29%					
	10-19%					
	0-9%					

Write your score in the correct level and then color in the graph to match your score. Then take out your calculator and add all five numbers and divide by 5. That is your average score for the week. Write that number here

_____%. Be sure to have your parents sign this paper each Friday and bring back on Monday.

The Four P's for Raising Self Esteem

Proficiency
(What skills are they lacking?)

Public Relations
(How can we make them look good?)

Student

Power
(How can we give them power over their emotions?)

Philanthropy
(How can we set them up to help others?)

Start Date: _____

Baseline grades _____

Baseline target behavior _____

Probe Date (one month later): _____

Probe grades _____

Triple T Chart

In order to see any behavior, change, we need to address the Triple T's.

Trigger	**Target**	**impacT**
Environmental Change/Cue	**Replacement Behavior**	**Response Feedback**

Triple T Chart

In order to see any behavior, change, we need to address the Triple T's.

Trigger	**Target**	**impacT**
Environmental Change/Cue	**Replacement Behavior**	**Response Feedback**

References

Alberto, P.A., Troutman, A.C. (1999). <u>Applied Behavior Analysis for Teachers</u>. Upper Saddle River: Prentice-Hall, Inc., 235-244.

Algozzine, B., Wang, C., White, R., Cooke, N., Duran, G., & Marr, M. (2012). Effects of multi-tier academic and behavior instruction on difficult-to-teach students. *Exceptional Children, 79*(1), 45-64. doi:10.1177/1098300709359084

Allday, R. A., Bush, M., Ticknor, N., & Walker, L. (2011). Using teacher greetings to increase speed to task engagement. *Journal of Applied Behavior Analysis, 44*(2), 393-396. doi:1011.1/2015.6307

Bambara, L., Knoster, T., & Browder, D. (1998). Designing positive behavior plans. Innovations. 13, 1-43.

Bandura, A. (2001). Social cognitive theory: An agentic perspective. *Annual review of psychology*. (Volume 52, pp 1-26). Palo Alto: Annual Reviews, Inc.

Ben-Sasson, A., Carter, A.S., & Briggs-Gowan, M.J. (2010). The development of sensory over-responsivity from infancy to elementary school. *Journal of Abnormal Child Psychology, 38*(8), 1193-1202. doi: 10.007/s10802-010-9435-9

Block, B. & Weatherford, G. (2013). Embodied Identities: Using Kinesiology Programming Methods to Diminish the Hegemony of the Normal. *Quest.* 65 (1), 31-43. Doi: 10.1080/00336297.2012.727370

Burgoyne, M.E., & Ketcham, C.J. (2015). Observation of classroom performance using therapy balls as a substitute for chairs in elementary school children. *Journey of Education and Training Studies, 3*(4), 42-48. doi:1105.13/549.072015

Cervellin, G., & Lippi, G. (2011). From music-beat to heart-beat: A journey in the complex interactions between music, brain and heart. *European Journal of Internal Medicine, 22*(4), 371-374. doi:10.426.1/1298.2011.675

Clemes, S. A., Barber, S. E., Bingham, D. D., Ridgers, N. D., Fletcher, E., Pearson, N., & ... Dunstan, D. W. (2015). Reducing children's classroom sitting time using sit-to-stand desks: findings from pilot studies in UK and Australian primary schools. *Journal of Public Health (Oxford, England),*

Commissaris, D. A., Könemann, R., Hiemstra-van Mastrigt, S., Burford, E., Botter, J., Douwes, M., & Ellegast, R. P. (2014). Effects of a standing and three dynamic workstations on computer task performance and cognitive function tests. *Applied Ergonomics, 45*1570-1578. doi:10.1016/j.apergo.2014.05.003

Davis, Ronald Dell. (1992) 37 Common Characteristics of Dyslexia. Retrieved July 1, 2016 from Davis Dyslexia Association International. Dyslexia the Gift website: http://www.dyslexia.com/?p=254.

Delavarian, M., Towhidkhah, F., Dibajnia, P., & Gharibzadeh, S. (2012). Designing a decision support system for distinguishing adhd from similar children behavioral disorders. *Journal of Medical Systems, 36*(3), 1335-1358. doi:10.1007/s10916-010-9594-9

Desrochers, M. N., Oshlag, R., & Kennelly, A. M. (2014). Using background music to reduce problem behavior during assessment with an adolescent who is blind with multiple disabilities. *Journal of Visual Impairment & Blindness, 108*(1), 31-66. doi:10.2652/4986.2014

Downing, J., & Eichinger, J. (2011). Instructional strategies for learners with dual sensory impairments in integrated settings. *Research and Practice for Persons with Severe Disabilities, 36*(3-4), 150-157. doi:10.2511/027494811800824471

Duncanson, E. (2014). Lasting effects of creating classroom space: A study of teacher behavior. *Educational Planning, 21*(3), 29-40.

Eisenman, G., Edwards, S., & Cushman, C. A. (2015). Bringing reality to classroom management in teacher education. *Professional Educator, 39*(1), 1-12. doi:10.2014/5467.9872.202014

Fedewa, A. L., & Erwin, H. E. (2011). Stability balls and students with attention and hyperactivity concerns: Implications for on-task and in-seat behavior. *American Journal of Occupational Therapy, 65*(4), 393-399. doi:10.5014/ajot.2011.000554

Ferreri, L., Aucouturier, J., Muthalib, M., Bigand, E., & Bugaiska, A. (2013). Music improves verbal memory encoding while decreasing prefrontal cortex activity: An fNIRS study. *Frontiers in Human Neuroscience, 71*. doi:10.3389/fnhum.2013.00779

Grubaugh, S., & Houston, R. (1990). Establishing a classroom environment that promotes interaction and improved student behavior. *Clearing House, 63*(8), 375-378. doi: http://eds.b.ebscohost.com.proxy1.ncu.edu/eds/detail/detail?vid=30&sid

Guardino, C. A., & Fullerton, E. (2010). Changing behaviors by changing the classroom environment. *Teaching Exceptional Children, 42*(6), 8-13. doi: http://eds.b.ebscohost.com.proxy1.ncu.edu/eds/pdfviewer/pdfviewer?sid=23f6f758-f654-4696-abaa-2ff15c7e0df8%40sessionmgr120&vid=33&hid=127

Hall, S. N., & Robinson, N. R. (2012). Music and reading: Finding connections from within. *General Music Today, 26*(1), 11-18. doi:10.1177/1048371311432005

Hannah, R. (2013). The effect of classroom environment on student learning. *Journal of Education Western Michigan University, 13*(1), 20-27. doi:10.143/2013.563

Hartanto, T. A., Krafft, C. E., Iosif, A. M., & Schweitzer, J. B. (2015). A trial-by-trial analysis reveals more intense physical activity is associated with better cognitive control performance in attention-deficit/hyperactivity disorder. *Child Neuropsychology: A Journal on Normal and Abnormal Development in Childhood and Adolescence*, 1-9.

Harvey, W., Wilkinson, S., Pressé, C., Joober, R., & Grizenko, N. (2014). Children say the darndest things: Physical activity and children with attention-deficit hyperactivity disorder. *Physical Education & Sport Pedagogy, 19*(2), 205-220.

Hattie, J. (2008). *Visible Learning: A synthesis of over 800 meta-analyses relating to achievement*. New York, NY: Routledge

Haydon, T., Conroy, M. A.; Scott, T. M., Sindelar, P. T., Orlando, A. (2010). A comparison of three types of opportunities to respond on student academic and social behaviors. Journal of Emotional and Behavioral Disorders, 18, 27-40.

Heiss, E. (2004). *Feng Shui for the classroom: 101 easy to use ideas*. Chicago, IL: Zephyr Press.

Horner, R. H., & Sugai, G. (2015). School-wide PBIS: An example of applied behavior analysis implemented at a scale of social importance. *Behavior Analysis in Practice*, *8*(1), 80-85. doi:10.1007/s40617-015-0045-4

Horner, R. H., Kincaid, D., Sugai, G., Lewis, T., Eber, L., Barrett, S., & Dickey, C. R. (2014). Scaling up school-wide positive behavioral interventions and support: Experiences of seven states with documented success. *Journal of Positive Behavior Interventions*, *16*(4), 197-208. doi:10.1177/1098300713503685

Imbeau, M., & Tomlinson, C. (2012). Leading and managing a differentiated classroom. *Journal of Exceptional Children*, *12*(1), 13-17. doi: 10.012/43978.03022012

Jaggi, P., Bakhshi, R., & Sandhu, P. K. (2013). Classroom furniture: How suitable for students. *Journal of Human Ecology*, *43*(3), 267.

Jensen, E. (2005). *Teaching with the Brain in Mind*. Alexandria, VA. ASCD

Kang, H. J., & Williamson, V. J. (2014). Background music can aid second language learning. *Psychology of Music*, *42*(5), 728-747. doi:10.1177/0305735613485152

Karadüz, A. (2010). Linguistic acts teachers use in the classroom: Verbal stimuli. *Education*, *130*(4), 696-704. doi:10.113/140.5647.032010

Keay-Bright, W., & Howarth, I. (2012). Is simplicity the key to engagement for children on the autism spectrum? *Personal & Ubiquitous Computing*, *16*(2), 129. doi:10.1007/s00779-011-0381-5

Kilbourne, J. (2011). Sharpening the mind through movement: Using exercise balls as chairs in a university class. *Research that Matters*, *3*, 3-9.

Küller R, Laike T. (1998). The impact of flicker from fluorescent lighting on well-being, performance and physiological arousal. *Ergonomics 41* (4): 433–47.

Lally P., van Jaarsveld C.H.M., Potts, H.W.W., Wardle J. (2010) How are habits formed: modelling habit formation in the real world. *European Journal of Social Psychology*. 40:998–1009.

Manolov, R., Gast, D. L., Perdices, M., & Evans, J. J. (2014). Single-case experimental designs: Reflections on conduct and analysis. *Neuropsychological Rehabilitation*, *24*(3/4), 634. doi:10.1080/09602011.2014.903199

Marzoli, D. & Tommassi L. (2009). Side biases in humans (Homo sapiens): Three Ecological Studies on Hemispheric Asymmetries. *Naturwissenschaften*, 96: 1099-1106.

Millei, Z. & Petersen, E.B. (2014). Complicating student behaviour: Exploring the discursive constitution of learner subjectivities. *Journal of Emotional and Behavioural Difficulties*, *20*(1), 20-34. doi:10.1080/13632752.2014.947097

National Education Association (NEA). (2013) Feng Shui: retrieved on February 1, 2014 http://www.nea.org/tools/feng-shui-for-the-classroom.html

Nelson, L. (2013). *Design and Deliver*. Baltimore, MD: Brookes Publishing.

Nuoffer, M. E. (2013). A case study on positive and relational discipline techniques. *Cognition, 119*(3), 394-402.

Oliver, R. M., Wehby, J. H., & Reschly, D. J. (2011). Teacher classroom management practices: Effects on disruptive or aggressive student behavior. *Campbell Collaboration Journal, 4*, 10-66. doi:10.4073/csr.2011.4

Pentland, J., Maciver, D., Owen, C., Forsyth, K., Irvine, L., Walsh, M., & Crowe, M. (2016). Services for children with developmental co-ordination disorder: An evaluation against best practice principles. *Disability & Rehabilitation, 38*(3), 299. doi:10.3109/09638288.2015.1037464

Perks, T., Orr, D., & Alomari, E. (2016). Classroom re-design to facilitate student learning: A case study of changes to a university classroom. *Journal of The Scholarship of Teaching & Learning, 16*(1), 53-68. doi:10.14434/josotl. v16i1.19190

Pfeiffer, B., Henry, A., Miller, S., & Witherell, S. (2008). Effectiveness of Disc 'o' Sit cushions on attention to task in second-grade students with attention difficulties. *American Journal of Occupational Therapy, 62*(3), 274-281.

Pfeiffer, B., Koenig, K., Kinnealey, M., Sheppard, M., & Henderson, L. (2014). Effectiveness of sensory integration interventions in children with autism spectrum disorders: A pilot study. *American Journal of Occupational Therapy, 65*(1), 76-85. doi:10.111/835030324

Prusak, K. A., & Barney, D. C. (2014). Skill progressions that maximize learning and motivation: Reflections for the classroom. *Global Journal of Health & Physical Education Pedagogy, 3*(1), 69. doi:10.127/834.2014

Ramli, N. H., Ahmad, S., & Masri, M. H. (2013). Improving the classroom physical environment: Classroom users' perception. *Procedia - Social and Behavioral Sciences, 101*, 221-229. doi:10.1016/j.sbspro.2013.07.195

Reinke, W.M., Stormont, M., Herman, K.C., Wang, Z., Newcomer, L., & King, K. (2014). Use of coaching and behavior support planning for students with disruptive behavior within a universal classroom management program. *Journal of Emotional and Behavioral Disorder, 22*(2), 74-82. doi:10.1177/1063426613519820

Rotz, R., & Wright, S. D. (2013). Fidget to focus: Outwit your boredom: Sensory strategies for living with ADD. New York, NY: Universe.

Safitry, T. S., Mantoro, T., Ayu, M. A., Mayumi, I., Dewanti, R., & Azmeela, S. (2015). Teachers' perspectives and practices in applying technology to enhance learning in the classroom. *International Journal of Emerging Technologies in Learning, 10*(3), 10-14. doi:10.3991/ijet.v10i3.4356

Sargeant, J. (2012). Qualitative Research Part II: Participants, Analysis, and Quality Assurance. *Journal of Graduate Medical Education, 4*(1), 1–3. http://doi.org/10.4300/JGME-D-11-00307.1

Schaaf, R. C., Benevides, T., Mailloux, Z., Faller, P., Hunt, J., van Hooydonk, E., ... Kelly, D. (2014). An intervention for sensory difficulties in children with autism: A randomized trial. *Journal of Autism and Developmental Disorders,44*(7), 1493–1506. doi:10.1007/s10803-013-1983-8

Schaaf, R. C., Schoen, S. A., May-Benson, T. A., Parham, L. D., Lane, S. J., Smith Roley, S., & Mailloux, Z. (2015). State of the science: A roadmap for research in sensory integration. *American Journal of Occupational Therapy, 69*(6), 1. doi:10.5014/ajot.2015.019539

Schoeberlen, D. (2009). *Mindful teaching and teaching mindfulness: A guide for anyone who teaches anything.* Boston, MA: Wisdom Publications.

Schult, T., Awosika, E., Schmunk, S., Hodgson, M., Heymach, B., & Parker, C. (2013). Sitting on stability balls: Biomechanics evaluation in a workplace setting. *Journal of Occupational and Environmental Hygiene, 10*(2), 55-63.

Schwabova, J. P., Maly, T., & Zahalka, F. (2015). Evaluation of peripheral and focal vision in proprioceptive differentiation of underfoot inversion angles: Comment on Witchalls, et al. (2013). *Perceptual and Motor Skills, 120*(2), 623-627. doi:10.2466/15.PMS.120v10x6

Shek, D. T., Sun, R. C., & Merrick, J. (2012). Positive youth development constructs: Conceptual review and application. *Scientific World Journal, 12,* 43-51. doi:10.1100/2012/152923

Shores, R., Gunter, P., & Jack, S. (1993). Classroom management strategies: Are they setting events for coercion? *Behavioral Disorders, 18,* 92–102.

Smith Roley, S., Mailloux, Z., Parham, L. D., Schaaf, R. C., Lane, C. J., & Cermak, S. (2015). Sensory integration and praxis patterns in children with autism. *American Journal of Occupational Therapy, 69*(1), 1-8. doi:10.5014/ajot.2015.012476

Tesh, J. (2013). Highlighting in orange causes cognitive awareness. Intelligence for your life. Radio broadcast.

Wang, H., Weiss, K., Haggerty, M., & Heath, J. (2014). The effect of active sitting on trunk motion. *Journal of Sport and Health Science, 3*(4), 333-337.

Wynkoop, K. (2016) Watch This! A Guide to Implementing Video Modeling in the Classroom. *Intervention in School and Clinic,* v51 n3 p178-183

*Some of the above references are in the PowerPoint presentation and not the booklet. In order to save printing costs, the booklet highlights the most important features.

www.ingramcontent.com/pod-product-compliance
Lightning Source LLC
Chambersburg PA
CBHW080600090426
42735CB00016B/3302